An Introduction to
Wedding Dress Alterations

Copyright © 2018 S. L. Harbour
All rights reserved.
ISBN-10: 1985204053
ISBN-13: 978-1985204058

An Introduction to
Wedding Dress Alterations

A Dressmaker's Guide to

Working with & Sewing Bridal Wear

S. L. Harbour

An Introduction to Wedding Dress Alterations.

Copyright ©2018 S. L. Harbour
Published by Deity an imprint of S. E. L. Harbour
Printed by CreateSpace

Cover design, text, layout, editing, and illustrations by S. L. Harbour

All rights reserved.

No part of this publication may be reproduced or transmitted in any form or by any means, electronic or mechanical including photocopying, recording or any information storage and retrieval system without permission in writing from the author except where by permitted by law.

Although every precaution has been taken in the preparation of this book, the author assumes no responsibility for errors or omissions. Neither is any liability assumed for damages or loss of earnings resulting from the use of the information contained herein.

The rights of S. L. Harbour to be identified as the author of this work have been asserted by her in accordance with the Copyright, Design & Patents Act 1988.

First Edition

Contents

A Bit of History	7
Before You Begin	11
The Art of Fitting a Bridal Gown	17
Understanding Figures	23
The Bridal Bodice	29
The Bridal Fabrics	35
Bridal Fastenings	41
Fitting Bodices	49
Fitting Hems	59
Fitting Figures	67
The Inner Workings of a Wedding Dress	85
The Boned Bodice	87
Combination Seams	95
Bindings	101
A Bit of Hand Sewing	107
And Sew to Sew	117
Glossary	119
About the Author	123
Other Titles	124

A Bit of History

A few decades ago bridal shops were typically owned and run by talented women (usually women) who had the ability to transform a flat pattern and a piece of fabric into a truly beautiful garment fit for a bride.

These women spent endless weeks creating sublime bridal gowns firstly for family and friends, and then as word spread of their abilities these women then went on to open their own boutiques with rails full of their own designs. I was fortunate to be offered a position at one of these boutiques and here I learnt my craft.

These shops were able to offer a personal service to their customers and deliver well-made and well fitted gowns drawing on their own unique aptitude and skill.

A number of these innovative dressmakers then went on to attract an exclusive clientele and thus 'designer bridal' was born.

With the arrival of imported clothing from the Far East came the heavily beaded bridal gowns. These gowns had a lot of man hours of beading, but due to the lower wages these dresses were surprisingly cheap to purchase and all too soon bridal manufacture moved.

A number of the smaller independent dressmakers realising the potential to offer more 'bling' for a greater profit margin and less working hours for themselves switched from creating their own gowns to buying in imported labels.

With most bridal shops today owned by people who will readily admit that '*I can't sew a button on,*' there is a real need for someone with the technical knowhow and the fearlessness to face any wedding gown.

Someone with the courage to look over a bride standing in her wedding dress and decide the best way to make the elaborate fabric fit like a couture creation.

Each season brings new designs and ideas to the bridal industry, and whilst at the college where I studied, the lecturers may raise a quizzical eyebrow at my methods, my subsequent years working with bridal gowns has seen many innovative ways to alter them. Not always employing traditional methods - sewing techniques are always evolving.

Bridal alterations are not complicated, they are time consuming and can be challenging. As a seamstress you will need to forget what you were perhaps taught at college or university or even what was taught within a hobby course.

Modern manufacturing methods have spawned a whole new perspective on the construction of garments. Many times it is up to the seamstress to conjure up an alternative but no less an effect way of altering a bridal gown to satisfy the demands of both the style and the figure.

Most bridal gowns produced in the Far East for established labels are created to a very high standard, with quality control paramount. The construction of the gowns has changed considerably with far less hand sewing on the main part of the garment but much more focus on the embellishments such as hand beading.

This has actually made the alteration process of these dresses far more straight forward.

However, necessity is the mother of invention and as a seamstress, creativity is our perpetual friend.

In some ways we are re-writing the traditional methods known to the tailors of old, building on their skills and developing and moving forward with new techniques of our own that can satisfy modern clothing.

With today's approach of trading overseas and importing everything from mobile phones to clothing it is interesting to note that there is one last bastion that cannot be imported –

The Seamstress.

Bridal gowns never have been, or ever will be returned to the manufacturer for alterations, it is simply not cost effective – *enter a talented group of individuals to fit, pin, unpick and stitch.*

In this Introduction to Wedding Dress Alterations I will be discussing the intricacies of bridal fittings and delving into some of the important sewing details.

This book offers a glimpse into the wonderful world of fitting and sewing bridal gowns.

For an in-depth study and to discover more, my full colour book *Bridal Alteration Techniques* is also available.

I do hope you enjoy your journey with me and I can spark your creativity into pursuing a career in bridal alterations.

The Bridal Industry needs You!

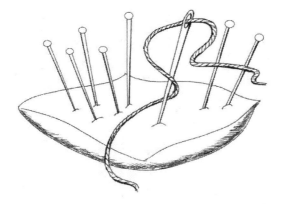

Before you begin

For the bridal seamstress there are a few need to knows whether you fit at your home, fit privately at a customer's home or work for bridal shops, like any profession you must be prepared for your appointments and have your 'tool box'.

These are your everyday essentials that you carry around with you. Obviously sewing machines will not be dragged to and from your work area, although I have on occasion taken mine.

Your sewing tool-box should have scissors, pins and pin cushions, tape measure, bust cups, wet wipes for freshening up your hands and possibly a kneeling pad for your knees.

You may also want a packet of plasters for the odd occasion when you need to stem the gush of blood that pours forth from your finger when you accidently stab it during the fitting.

If fitting at a shop and the final fitting is complete all but a last minute detail to hand stitch then of course there will also be needles, thread, press studs, ribbon, hooks and bars, buttons and blue bows to fit into your sewing kit.

Fitting times

Ideally bridal fittings should commence 8 -10 weeks prior to the wedding day. This is usually the optimum time allocated by the bridal industry.

This fits into the bridal diary and allows for any problems when arranging appointments; needless to say March through to mid-September is a demanding time in the diary of any bridal seamstress.

It has been known for last minute bridal gown fittings and alterations to be turned around within 24 hours. This is obviously an extreme time frame and quite simply puts undue pressure on both the bride and the seamstress and leaves no room for any unexpected problems that may arise.

Hence bridal fittings tend to be spread over weeks rather than days.

This ensures hen weekends, work commitments, holidays and childcare to name but a few aspects of everyday life and indeed the wedding day can be accommodated comfortably.

It also needs to be pointed out that as well as fitting the dress the seamstress must also have the time to sew the said item too.

For the first fitting the bride should have purchased her foundation garments such as her bra or basque and underskirts if required and indeed her shoes.

Sometimes though, things do not always go according to plan. The shoes may not have materialised or the bride was perhaps waiting to consult with a seamstress on what foundation garments were actually needed.

These things happen – hence the reason why fittings are scheduled so far in advance.

Pricing & Estimates

A quick internet search will offer a reasonable guide to pricing bridal alterations. If ever there saying 'how long is a piece of string' was more relevant then it can be paraphrased to 'how long will it take to sew on a few beads?'

The truth is with such variants to work with it is not quite as simple as quoting to shorten a pair of jeans.

Generally the reason a seamstress will be chosen for a bridal alteration will be because she has been recommended for the job.

A bride will very rarely phone around for the cheapest quote. Neither will a bride invite a seamstress to pop by whilst she stands in her dress, just for the seamstress to take a short intake of breath and with a shake of the head declare it to be a big job such as the proverbial plumber or mechanic might.

Only when the dress is viewed along with the individual wearing it can prices be quoted. In my experience brides will not skimp on achieving the perfect fitting dress.

For this reason *always itemise* each alteration this way brides have all the facts about how much work is actually involved and ensure the time spent fitting is also included. Whether there is an individual price or just an overall price, this is your choice.

Taking in side seams or hollowing out the back on a beaded dress can actually be three procedures at least and is not simply a case of '...it just needs taking in a bit...'

A lace hem will have multiple layers of foundation skirts as well as the complete removal of an edging lace, again more than '...it just needs a bit off the bottom...' it really is only when brides take a closer look at their gown and realise it is quite an involved area of sewing.

With so many combinations of fabric, styles, body shapes and beadwork it is little wonder many seamstresses are underpaid for the jobs they take on.

When you begin to factor in the traveling expenses and insurance aspect plus general overheads then offering a quote over the phone is nigh impossible.

Is there a fitting charge involved? Is this extra or is it factored into the price?

A number of shops will happily fit a garment for a set price allowing the individual to take the garments elsewhere to be altered. So this is not a rarity as you may initially believe, yet it is a little overlooked element.

Having a separate and defined fitting charge may in fact give your job more kudos and respect; you are after all providing a very specialised and professional service.

Consider a comparison with another element of the beauty industry – hairdressing. Many brides will employ the services of a hairdresser for the special day and indeed have a hair trial or perhaps a personal trainer? The latter would be paid by the hour, why then shouldn't you? After all your job does not finish when the bride leaves your company, you are providing a professional, personal service in the form of fitting the garment, just like the hairdresser or personal trainer.

One important note on the subject of paperwork – do not forget to organise adequate insurance.

How much cover you will need depends on your working environment, at the very least the insurance will need to cover you for the work you undertake if you work as a self-employed person.

It's All About Me

Perhaps something that might be overlooked is your own attire, the way you dress the way you present yourself to others.

As a seamstress involved with such precious garments is it imperative that the right impression is given.

Turning up in scruffy jeans and a t shirt may work perfectly well for dog walking or gardening occupations but brides and their guests will be expecting a high level of professionalism.

Do think about comfort as crawling around on your hands and knees pinning hems is not glamorous, so wearing a slim fitting or short skirt is perhaps best avoided.

Flexibility, so this is not just when and where you can undertake your fitting appointments, but also your own physique. Wedding dresses are heavy and you will need to be constantly lifting and positioning the train – I call it *'flouffing'*. Not a technical term or a real word but brides like the idea that they can appoint a *'chief flouffer'*.

Once again working on hems you will spend a great deal of time on the floor, checking and pinning so you may want to practice your Yoga!

A beautifully tailored jacket may well look the part, but for bending, stretching and lifting heavy gowns from rails it may restrict your efforts the last thing you need is the sound of tearing seams as you zip up the gown.

Keep jewellery to the minimum, long necklaces will simply cause a nuisance and steer clear of bracelets and rings with set stones mounted with claws as these will pluck at delicate lace and tulle.

Do not wear too much make up as you will be working close to the fabric and it will easily transfer if you should brush against it.

This is perhaps the most important rule – *never, ever, ever* wear lipstick when fitting frocks, especially as like most seamstresses the third hand is the mouth. This is where health and safety goes out of the window and pins will go between the lips.

The Bill

No-one likes asking for money even when it has been for a job well done and it is money owed. It is however a necessity and as such an invoice should be prepared for your customer.

A disclaimer should also be included and signed by the bride. This simply covers areas such as strange antics the bride may do in her dress like sky diving and exuberant dancing etc., it is after all a wedding dress and may not be suitable for some 21st century jaunts.

In theory the bridal shop should really give the bride 'lessons on how to be a bride'.

It isn't every day that a person wears an expensive frock so it is important that the bride realises that in order to wear a heavily boned bodice with a long skirt and train, she will require a little more in the way of graceful behaviour.

The Art of Fitting a Bridal Gown

The secret of looking good is having a garment that fits beautifully. Naturally the Wedding Dress is **THE** gown that has to fit to perfection.

When a gown is made to measure by a professional couturier then this is always achievable as each stage of the garment construction revolves around a fitting with the customer to ensure each seam and stitch complies with what is expected of the given style.

The majority of bridal gowns will be manufactured to a standard size and will need the expertise of a seamstress to achieve a good fit.

The Art of Conversation

Fitting bridal gowns can be classed as a bit of an art form. The various body shapes teamed with the ever changing styles and pattern blocks used to create the gorgeous gowns on offer can almost be deemed classic enough to sit beside a Rembrandt, *well maybe not.*

There is more to fitting a bridal dress than simply sticking pins into a piece of fabric. Along with all of the other details when fitting a garment the most important factor is the customer.

It is your job not only to fit the gown to an acceptable standard but an aspect overlooked with most seamstresses is to communicate with your bride.

Ask her how she feels in her gown. What are her expectations? Is the bride imagining her double DD's to be fully contained or does she want to go for the full Nell Gwyn effect with a heaving bosom?

Is she expecting to walk in a mermaid gown that she wants taking in so tight at the knees that performing even the most basic of tasks is likely to end up on some reality TV program or worse the internet? Does your bride intend on arriving on horseback – wearing a sheath style dress?

So many options you need to be aware of, without conversing with your bride you will not know how best to move forward with the fitting. Fitting a bridal gown is all about finding the right solution for any problem that arises. If the problem is with the fit then that is something you have to adjust.

Equally if the problem is with what the bride is expecting from her dress such as horseback riding or trudging up Ben Nevis in her wellies then tact and diplomacy are something you must also have in your sewing kit too!

The Changing Room

As with all bespoke professions that require the personal touch stepping into a changing room with a complete stranger is quite a daunting task, both for the customer and the expert.

Confidence and consideration are two key factors when working with the bridal party. The bride needs to be assured that her modesty will be upheld in the highest degree and that under no circumstances will her bottom poke out from behind the curtain whilst she is in a state of undress.

It is your responsibility as the professional to exude an air of composure whilst in these confines and to direct the customer to what is required of her

Foundations

When a bride choses her bridal gown it is obviously a huge decision, but once chosen everything else will either fall into place or set stress levels to a *code red* when it comes to choosing shoes and underwear, not to mention other important accessories such as jewellery, veils, flowers, tiaras etc.

Many brides when they think of their wedding trousseaux will naturally think of something gorgeous silky soft, edged with Chantilly lace and they will not be expecting it to be worn for too long.

This is lingerie; it is sexy, romantic and totally unsuitable for wearing under a bridal gown.

Brides will quite often expect a great deal from their gown, sometimes more than the dress is able to deliver. They may refer constantly to the image they've seen and simply wish to emulate this ethereal ideal of the prefect bride. We as seamstresses must where ever possible attempt to supply as much as we can to aid this vision of loveliness.

The way we can do this is with foundation garments. These are not usually pretty, not sexy but they will lift, squeeze and hold most wobbly boobs, bums and tums. From stick on bras to *belly-smacker knickers* that will smooth and flatten, Mother Nature may have failed her daughter but there will usually be a man-made alternative.

Many bridal gowns are produced with a plentiful supply of boning allowing the bride to be pulled and shaped but this boning is only as good or supportive as the fastenings. There does come a point when the zipper gives up, the buttons pop off or the corset loops abandon all hope.

So when the bride demands that the gown is pulled in tighter or the seams be taken in another 2 cms, gently remind her of the fastenings and the stresses they will be under.

Dressing the Bride

On the day of the wedding the bride will have had her hair and makeup applied, so during fittings encourage the bride to step into her gown so she is accustomed to this method of dressing.

There will of course always be exceptions to this, for example a pear shaped figure may struggle.

No shoes should be worn for this initial part; this allows the bride to feel for the floor and avoids the issue of snagging the dress with either the heels or any fastenings.

I like to tell my brides that they are the queen for the day and that they should allow her attendants to undertake the menial tasks.

Additional underskirts should be placed on the floor first with the gown then placed over it. Hooped petticoats will create a 'well' for the bride to step into. Allow the bride to pull up the underskirt whilst you in turn raise the gown. Check if the gown has a waist stay and fasten this on the tightest hook.

Assess whether the gown is sitting correctly over bust area, this may alter the position of the waist stay. Once the underskirt and waist stay are in position the gown can be fastened

Have the bride place her hands on her natural waistline at her sides and begin with the zip or the buttons from the bottom upwards, a gentle squeeze from the bride at the waist will ease the zip or buttons over snug areas such as waist seams.

Continue to fasten, once level with the bust area, ask the bride to lift her bosom into the princess seams of the gown, even if the bosom appears to be high it will 'find its own level' just like water. Pushing the shoulders back also helps when fastening a gown.

Zipper fastenings have the advantage of a small hook and bar at the top of the zipper this is useful when finishing the last section of the zip.

Gowns with internal corsets such as couture gowns can have these laced to assess the fit. If the two edges of the corset meet or overlap then the gown is too big.

The corset should not be fastened at this fitting, instead the gown will need to be assessed to determine how much will need to be taken and from where.

Lace up gowns will need the corseting to start from the top, loop the cord through the rouleaux loops loosely at first. At the waist line begin to tighten each piece of lattice, as it becomes tighter ask the bride to lift her bosom into position. Continue to lace the bodice.

The Fitting Process

Fitting the bodice should be the first procedure undertaken; if the bodice is not sitting in the correct position the hem cannot be successfully fitted.

Standard dressmaking pins are not always suitable when fitting bridal bodices due to the structure. Longer dressmaking pins with a shaft length of 5cms are favoured or larger safety pins.

You will need to advise your customer that you are using pins, yes it is obvious but brides can become quite excited and forget, so remind them if they move around too much during the fitting.

Foundation garments will need to have been purchased by the bride if they intend to wear them; these include a basque, strapless bra or a bra that has invisible straps. If required any additional petticoats.

In many bridal gowns the structure and boning is usually sufficient therefor foundation garments are rarely needed. Generally the gown is intended to be so closely fitted to the body that wearing additionally boned items causes more of an irritation and is usually dispensed with in favour of bust cups.

Bust cups offer a modest lift as well as increasing the cup size when fitted to gowns. Couture cups or bust cups can be purchased widely and come in various colours, ivory or flesh tones are the best to use in bridal alterations. Couture cups will be contoured so they are slim at the top and fuller at the bottom

If the bride requires a little more cleavage rather than fullness then the cups can be trimmed down to create a 'fillet' that can be stitched to the gown to offer a 'lift'. But the gown itself must fit tightly around the bust area for these to work.

Bust cups however are not sufficient to offer a lift in gowns that have zero support for example backless dresses or gowns that have a low décolletage. Here specialised foundation garments will need to be purchased.

This is especially important for larger cup sizes where the gown is low cut. If the bride has been well advised by the shop then this should not be an issue, her needs will have been discussed and the correct style of gown should have been chosen.

During the first and possibly second fitting it is important that you caution your bride about 'trying everything on'. This will be best left for the final fitting.

There is a lot going on during the first couple of fittings and a great deal of moving around and sharp pins to consider. If your bride is wearing a veil then she will obviously wish to see how her outfit all comes together. This should be tried on when there is no danger of snagging on a stray pin.

Understanding Figures

Bridal manufacturers will all work from what is called a Block – this is basically their impression of what the perfect proportions of bust, waist and hip ratio should be.

This will usually be on a slight 'Pear Shape' with the hip measurement somewhat larger than the bust. They will have their own tailor's dummy that is made or padded to their size 12. From this they will then make what is called a 'block' pattern and they will use this to make any dress pattern in their design range. This pattern is then graded up or graded down from the original size 12. Needless to say they do not accommodate for all figures types of which there are four.

The Four Figure Types

For the average size female then there are four main body shapes, the Apple, The Pear, The Hourglass and the Straight figure types.

The 'average' aspect here is principally the basic shape of an individual who is of average height and of average weight.

Once we delve into the realms of plus sizes then this is where the plethora of body shapes will undoubtedly come into play. Hormonal fluctuations, pregnancy and breast implants will also expand on the ever growing 'body shape' deliberations.

Knowing the basic four body shapes will help to guide the seamstress in the right direction of what to look for during the fitting process.

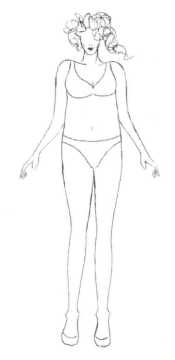

The Apple Shaped Figure

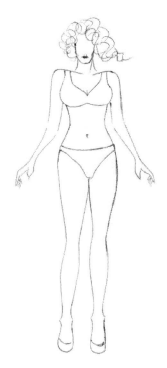

The Hourglass Figure

The Apple Shaped Figure

The apple body form has an ample bosom with a thicker waistline, legs are slender and hips narrow.

This gown will need the bust darting to accommodate the fuller cup size or if the waist is fuller then the front side seams will need taking in; the waist may need letting out and the upper hips will need to be taken in.

Gowns ordered for this body shape will be based on the waist measurement which will be generous in proportion to the hips. Check that the centre back sits correctly below the waistline due to narrow hips.

The Hourglass Shaped Figure

The hourglass figure type is the envy of most women due to the corseted figure ideals of history. The hourglass figure resembles the traditional egg-timer with the bust and hips of similar proportions and the waist in contrast quite neat and small.

As the bust and hips are similar in size the wedding dress will have been ordered to fit either of these, the A Line gown or full skirted dress will still need to accommodate the fuller bust area.

Darts may be needed to accommodate the fuller cup size and the waist will usually need to be taken in.

Taking in from the centre back to curve into a 'sway back' may be an alternative adjustment to the side seam as some body curves can cause the side seam to pull if taken in too much.

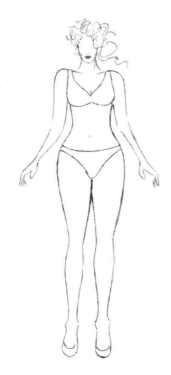

The Pear Shaped Figure

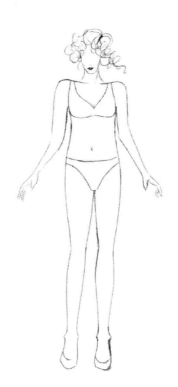

The Straight Figure

Pear Shaped Figure

The pear shaped figure type is a well-known body shape, and one most commonly used for pattern drafting, here the bust is relatively small compared to the hips but the waist is small.

As most bridal size charts work on a slight pear shape figure generally these gowns require very little in the way of alterations to the bodice especially for a fuller skirted or an A line gown as this could be ordered in a size appropriate to the bust and waist measurements.

Depending on bust to waist ratio the bust may need taking in from the front and additional bust cups may be required.

Subject to the gown shape a larger size may be needed to accommodate hips, styles such as fishtails, here the gown will need to be taken in on the bust and waist area.

The Straight Figure Shape

The straight figure has a lithe build with very few curves. The bust area is modest and the hips slender. The waist line is not clearly defined.

Alterations will include bust cups and possibly taking in at the bust area. The hips will also need to be taken in.

Dresses ordered for this figure shape will be based on the waistline measurement which will be generous in proportion to the bust and hips.

As with the apple shape check that the centre back below the waistline is flat against the back this may need taking in from this area.

A well-fitting bodice should have smooth lines without wrinkles, knowing where to alleviate these wrinkles is not simply a case of pinning them in a hap-hazard way.

The seamstress must understand why the wrinkles are there and how to eliminate them using either traditional methods or creative techniques.

Yes it is important that the gown looks exactly as the manufacturer created it, but the factory used a standard block and pattern and not a real live person.

If a dart here or there would improve the fit, then don't be afraid of working a dart into the design. *Just because the designer didn't put a dart there doesn't mean one cannot be used.*

Only a small proportion of the population actually conform to the manufacturers size chart, inevitably the gown will need altering to fit the individual, hence why us seamstresses are never out of work.

Wedding dresses on the whole tend to be on the smaller side of the measurement spectrum. So for example the high street size 12 will usually conform to a wedding dress size 14.

Physiologically speaking this isn't tremendous news for any woman. There is also the added confusion of ordering a USA size 12 as this would be a UK size 14.

The Bridal Bodice

Wedding dresses are exquisitely created works of art. What makes them so effortlessly glamorous is the use of the boning and in some dresses copious amounts of it are used.

In general, bridal gowns will employ the uses of boning, some more than others. It does not necessarily follow that the more expensive the gown the more construction it will have, some mass produced bridal gowns can have up to 40 pieces of boning stitched into them – I know, I've altered a great number of them.

The test for any seamstress is the application of boning into a garment. The supreme test for any artisan is to apply boning successfully into a bridal gown.

With the invention of sew-in boning bridal wear has been permitted to experiment where fashion has laid waste to corsetry – bridal gowns can now venture into the for-front of design and re-shape the nation's waistlines.

Gone are the stays, thrown out by the suffragettes and world wars but the same desire to be restricted and formed to an ideal of womanhood is the aspiration of many brides at whatever age. The whale boned corsets have long been disregarded in every-day fashion yet still women have felt the desire to don a corset for their wedding day.

There are two main construction techniques used for manufacturing bridal gowns: the Manufactured and the Couture. The main difference is that on one the stitching securing the boning is visible on the other it is not.

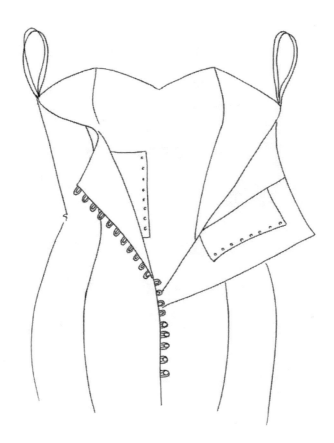

The Couture Bodice

The Couture Bodice

The couture bodice takes inspiration from the original boned corsets of yester-year; their structure and the fit are superb.

This is primarily due to the toiles that would have been created for the design, whether it is a made to measure or a capsule collection available to the bridal shops.

The bodice is created by first preparing a corset structure that mirrors the shape and size of the design. This corset is made from heavy weight cotton known as 'collar and cuff canvas' as you might imagine its original intended use was for mounting collars and cuffs in shirts.

This corset is then boned with careful attention to keep the boning running in smooth straight lines. The only curves will be over the front princess seams.

The fashion fabric is stitched, pressed and then stretched over the corset and secured along the neckline, if necessary also along the waist. The fashion fabric is essentially mounted over the corset and forms a ridged structure.

A loose lining is then stitched to the upper edges of the dress offering a professional finish to the inside of the gown, no boning or stitching is visible.

An internal eyeletted corset may also be added for extra support. This will be stitched into the back princess seams.

Couture gowns will usually be fastened with handmade rouleau loops and tiny covered buttons. Some couture gowns may even have a zip hidden beneath for extra strength.

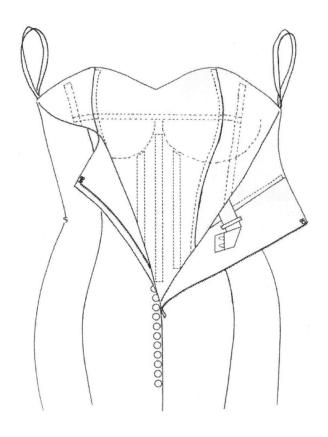

The Mass-produced Bodice

The Mass-produced Bodice

This is the most widely used method of construction in bridal gowns. This originated from the Far Eastern factories.

Gowns produced in factories undergo the same design development as couture wedding dresses but to minimise costs they have been developed a way to supply a cost effective superior finish whilst still retaining the important elements of the couture bodice. Boning is the key component teamed with a good foundation and pattern cutting.

Many of the best manufactures put just as much time and effort into their structure as the couture designers but are able to offer more in the way of additional beadwork and 'bling' to their customers for a very similar if not cheaper price tag.

There is just as much boning if not more to be found in manufactured gowns. The main identifying feature of the manufactured corset is the visibility of the boning stitches.

Because of this feature these bodices need to ensure the stitching is incredibly neat at the fabric used to support them is of good quality.

Many manufactures will use heavy weight duchesse satin – this sounds expensive but during the pattern lay and cutting process there will be ample 'off cuts' that can be used.

The outer shell of the gown sits over the 'corset' which is essentially the lining. Boning is attached directly onto the lining with stitch lines showing through on the right side.

The combinations of boning techniques used for this method of construction are endless. These range from each seam fitted with boning to insertions of boning between the seams, boning can also be used to curve around the bust area and across the bust line.

Couture cups - shaped pieces of foam padding are sometimes stitched over the bust area of the princess seam, sandwiched between the fashion fabric and the lining, this gives a very smooth line over the bust area and holds the shape of the bodice.

Internal corsets are seldom used for these gowns but waist stays made from elastic are often added and stitched into the side seams.

Manufactured gowns will typically have a zipper to fasten; using either a standard or concealed variety. With a small hook and bar to secure at the closure of the zip.

A relatively new addition to the fastening is the lattice back. Here rouleaux loops are fitted down the centre back of the gown and a length of satin cord is used to create a corset or lattice fastening. Again the satin will be readily available and there is no need for a zipper, buttons, an eyelet machine or hand finishing.

Buttons and handmade rouleau loops are seldom used although buttons as a design feature and elasticated loops are becoming more popular. These are used to fasten cuffs and illusion necklines (an upper bodice made of tulle).

There is no right or wrong way of applying boning to garments. Quite simply some techniques work better than others and knowing the various procedures is the key to understanding how to fit and how to alter a bridal gown successfully.

The Bridal Fabrics

Each generation will have an opinion of the best and most desirable fabrics that should be used to make bridal gowns. Silk, corded lace, chiffon, taffeta or damask the choice and plethora of gorgeous fabrics is never ending.

The fact is in the 21st century there are literally 1000's of fabrics from which designers and manufacturers can choose to create stunning wedding gowns here are just a few of them.

Silk: Made from the cocoon of the silk moth it has long been a mainstay for those wishing to indulged in the most finest of fabrics. From the Emperors of China to modern day brides the wearing of silk is synonymous with wealth.

During WWII parachutes were gathered up by women to use the fine silk to create their underwear, such was the versatility of the fibre. Now silk manufacturers design every conceivable style of fabric and use this natural fibre in the process and not necessarily the very sheer.

It is woven into organza, dupion, duchesse satin, chiffon, tulle, crepe, suiting, jacquard, damask and Habuti it is truly a versatile medium one that permits the body to breathe and it has the ability to keep the person warm.

The most popular silk in bridal wear is dupion, a slubby textured weave sometimes referred to as raw silk, duchesse satin (see above on satin fabrics), chiffon, organza and crepe, all gorgeous in their own right.

Satin: A luxurious fabric specifically woven to offer a beautiful lustre and sheen with a smooth finish. Most people when they think of bridal wear will think of this type of fabric, they think of satin and usually refer to it as silk.

The most common satin fabrics are duchesse satin this is a heavy weight satin and can be manufactured either from polyester or silk or a combination of both.

Next there is the lighter weight satin such as slipper satin this is what conjures up visions of expensive lingerie, again available in silk and polyester but also as a very light weight acetate. The latter is often used for lining in coats and jackets.

The term satin also transcends to other fabrics too such as satin backed crepe, satin organza, satin backed shantung, double sided satin, matt satin the list can go on it simply refer to the lustre and the weave that creates the fabric.

Mikado/zibeline: An incredibly firm fabric similar to suiting fabric with a distinct grain like denim. The polyester version is referred to as Mikado whilst the silk is called zibeline this fabric cannot be folded as a permanent crease will form and cannot be removed.

Dupion: mainly produced in silk has a slubby texture, the polyester version of this is called shantung and is usually satin backed.

Crepe: not just an enjoyable pancake but also a style of fabric with a distinct crimped weave that can also have a slight satin finish to the wrong side.

Habotai: a very light weight fabric sometimes called China Silk commonly used for printing scarves, used in bridal for linings.

Taffeta: A crisp light weight fabric has a very 'plastic' sound when handled.

Chiffon: A soft, transparent fabric flows and drapes well but a most evil fabric to work with.

Georgette: A fabric very similar to chiffon only slightly heavier in weight often referred to as chiffon.

Organza: Another transparent fabric but with slightly more body than chiffon will fray easily but will drape and move beautifully.

Tulle and net these are both 'knitted structures' and can either be a hexagonal knit or diamond knit. The weights of these two fabrics can vary considerably.

Heavy net is most commonly used for underskirts, here it is gathered and creates petticoats sometimes single tiers or multiple tiers with multiple layers depending on the style required.

Lighter weight net or tulle is often used as backing for full skirts to offer stability and fullness.

Tulle is mostly reserved for veils where it is gathered onto a comb and decorated with beads, crystals, lace. Lace edging looks stunning around the hem of a veil creating what is known as a Mantilla veil, popular in Spanish bridal couture.

Netting or tulle do not fray they can be left as a simple cut edge or a simple pencil edge can be stitched using an over locked 'rolled' hem.

Tulle is a relatively inexpensive fabric so many factories have been utilising it to create full skirted bridal gowns. These gorgeous gowns have multiple layers of tulle and have a very romantic look.

Netting is usually made from nylon whereas tulle can be made in polyester, nylon or silk, veils made from silk being very popular, delicate and extremely expensive.

Lace: Traditionally lace was referred to by the place of manufacture such as Chantilly, Alencon, Nottingham, Italian etc.

Lace is characterised by what is called the 'ground', 'net' background or 'mesh' that holds the fabric together.

These are too numerous to discuss here but lace in itself is a fascinating subject to pursue, but basically for the bridal industry they fall into four categories:

Chantilly - a delicate all over patterned lace with a very fine net background and lavish detail.

Guipure - densely patterned heavy lace with pieces connected by small plaits or threads rather than netting.

Corded - a raised outline of couched stitches holding the cord in position over the lace defining the detail.

Embroidered tulle - as the name implies this is classed as lace but it is in fact tulle that has been embroidered.

There are many variations of these laces, some expensive and used by top end bridal designers the price reflects the manufacturing country and technique used, many mainstream manufactured laces are very competitively priced

Along with the familiar laces used manufacturers also use a copious amount of lace applique, lace edging and beaded lace.

Depending on the manufacturer beaded detail may be done prior to the application, this makes altering relatively stress free as the removal of applique will not involve re-beading the motifs.

Lace edging can either produced as a separate entity or when using lace pieces then usually one or both of the selvedges will be finished with a scalloped edge. This generally trimmed from the main fabric during cutting and production then utilised afterwards. Mantilla Lace veils are having a revival, popular in Spain these gorgeous veils are trimmed with lace edging.

Most manufactured gowns that are termed lace are in fact a series of appliqued motifs stitched onto a tulle base. This offers the factory a simple yet dramatic way of using cheaper lace motifs as an alternative.

In Far East manufacturer the labour cost is considerably cheaper than the fabric costs, hence the applique although time consuming is, for factories the cheaper option. It is also a superb way of ensuring the gown has 'mirror' image pattern match throughout.

Lace is always an expensive medium to work with and inevitably will produce a considerable amount of waste. Instead of using vast quantities of lace by the metre the factories will use the motifs and applique these onto the gowns.

Jacquard, Damask and Brocade: These fabrics are quite easy to confuse but essentially they are pattered woven fabrics created with different weaving techniques.

Jacquard: uses a special loom attachment essentially like a punch card used for knitting machines; this refers to the technique used rather than the actual fabric.

Modern computerised techniques have advanced this practice but it is really the same method.

Brocade: can be distinguished by looking at the reverse here you will find a messy wrong side with either the weft threads cut or left to 'float'.

Damask: fabric is principally reversible - the same on both the wrong side and the right side and due to the weave of plain, twill or sateen the whole fabric will shimmer.

Bridal Fastenings

Throughout history of humans covering their bodies there has always been the need for the fastening of these garments. A piece of twine, a belt, a brooch, lacing, buttons and in the 20th century the zipper was invented by Gideon Sundback (although the zipper did have its debut in Chicago in 1893).

The Zipper.

A long standing fastening for the fashion industry the zipper is still used extensively in bridal gowns. These are either the standard zipper where the zipper has a flap covering it or the concealed zip, although not as firm as the standard zip it does offer a smooth finish.

The use of hook and bars at the upper edge of the zip offers a final anchor for any zipper. But under too much stress they are prone to breaking, so where-ever possible replace with a heavy duty size.

Although bridal gowns are considered a delicate item of clothing the zipper is generally a sturdier affair. But care should always be taken when fitting bridal gowns to ensure the dress fits comfortably so as not to rupture the zipper. Any forcing of the zip into closure can result in the teeth splitting and the zip breaking.

A good practice is to ask the bride to place her hands on her waist and gently squeeze, this will to offer a little 'ease'. This extra 'ease' will enable the zip to glide into position, this is especially important if the gown has a waist seam as the bulk of the seam can cause problems.

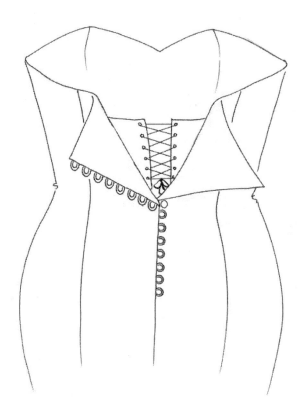

Buttons, Loops & internal Corset

Buttons and Loops

Couture bridal gowns favour rouleau loops and covered buttons to fasten.

Rouleaux are narrow strips of bias fabric that are stitched to create a dainty channel, and then turned through to form a fabric cord. (They are not complicated to make but can be fiddly to pull through). The loops themselves are generally of a good firm thickness to offer a secure loop.

Covered buttons have made an unprecedented come back onto the bridal market both for manufactured gowns and couture. These can be stitched onto the gown as functional fastening or simply as a design feature. The spacing for these buttons will vary from designer to designer.

Elasticated loops have recently been introduced to accompany a zipper fastening. These are manufactured pieces of braid that have been created with loops of sheering elastic.* Working alongside the zipper they loops will flick over buttons to conceal the zip teeth.

A crochet hook is usually recommended to the bride and her attendant to help with fastening.

*A number of gowns have seen this introduced by way of a delicate closure, on illusion tulle necklines and lace, however these do not offer a secure fastening, especially as the gown would need to be tightly fitted.

The elastic stretches and will eventually break. Replacing them with loops made from either lining fabric or tulle is the better option.

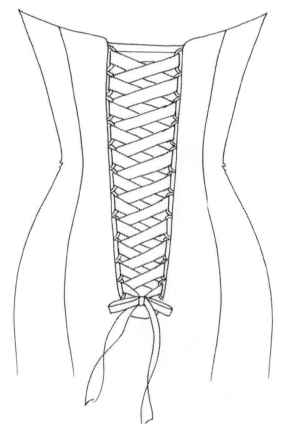

The Lattice Back Corset

Corseting

Always a traditional method of closure for many gowns throughout the centuries the corset backed gown has recently become a staple for modern bridal dresses.

Brides love the idea of a gown that 'sucks them in' and offers an hourglass silhouette. The fact is with expert pattern cutting and a copious amount of boning this can be achieved without a corset back.

There are a couple of styles used for lacing bridal gowns and both disciplines of corset backs will generally need a modesty panel to sit beneath the lacing. Some styles may have a removable upper panel in order to view the lattice.

The Rouleaux or Lattice Back Corset

A more recent addition to the bridal fastening repertoire is the lattice back.

The lattice back fastening is perhaps the most resourceful of the corset style fastenings as it does not require the machinery needed for eyelet application.

Here the centre back is cut slightly smaller from the upper edge grading down to a slight curve at the bottom. This is to allow the rouloux loops to sit apart and form the decorative lattice feature.

Due to the excess pressure the rouleaux loops used for these closures are constructed slightly differently than standard loops and so are considerably stronger.

A lattice back bodice is relatively straightforward to create and therefor in bridal shop circles it is a valuable skill for a seamstress to have.

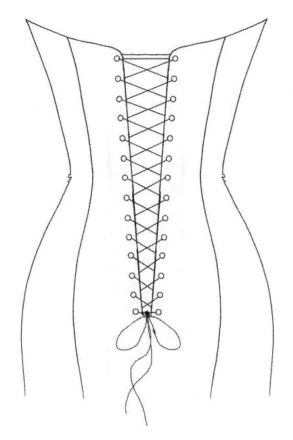

The Eyelet Back Corset

The Eyelet Back Corset

Reminiscent of Tudor gowns this style of corset fastening is based on the lacing of traditional corsets.

The eyelet technique can be fitted to the centre back of the gown and often will be heavily boned down the centre back edge.

Dresses with these eyelets can be worn edge to edge with no visible gap between or as in the lattice back gown worn slightly open to show either the modesty panel or bare flesh if desired.

It should be noted that the eyelets used for these gowns must be created by machine. There are a number of eyelet components available in many haberdashery outlets, but due to the immense strain these are unsuitable for bridal wear.

There are specialist companies who will apply eyelets to your garments. These come in various sizes and colours to suit your garment.

Internal Corsets and the Waist Stay.

In addition to the standard fastenings of bridal gowns there is also the use of internal components to secure the bridal bodice. A number of bridal gowns will have additional corsets or an elasticated waist stay to give support.

For the couture gowns small eyelet corsets can be inserted into the back princess seams of the lining and anchored to the main bodice. This allows the corset to be pulled securely without distorting the bodice.

These will pull tight and offer a good support on the waist, especially important for bustier gowns the bride will need to feel secure and that the bodice will not slip down.

Another type of internal corset is the *waist stay*. In historical costumes this would have been a length of twill tape that would wrap around the waist line and prevent the gown from wandering.

In modern gowns this has been replaced with elastic and bra fastening hooks and bars. These 'half belts' are generally stitched into the side seams and secured through loops along the princess seams.

They come in various widths from 3.5cms to 12-15 cms. Technically speaking the narrow width is the better format as the hooks and bar fastening on a deeper waist stay cannot conform to a waist and rib cage shape the way an eyelet corset would.

That said plus sized gowns will benefit from the wider waist stay as the tummy area and rib cage are of similar proportions.

Fitting Bodices

When it comes to fitting a bridal bodice there are five main areas that will need to be looked at, *if the gown is a bustier then there are only three areas.*

Most commercially manufactured bridal gowns are graded to a C cup and manufacturers labour extensively on achieving the perfect shaped bust seam, so unless the gown requires to be downsized by more than 6 inches the princess seam should not be altered.

However this is all relative to the size of gown. For example plus sized gowns can be taken in more at the side seams as usually proportions will change and offer slightly more flexibility to the downsize alteration.

The Bust:

Check that the bosom is 'sitting' in the correct position. For boned bodices this will need the bust lifting and allowed to fall into the princess seam. Fitting the bust area will depend on the bride's bust cup proportions in relation to the gown size and also her height, a petit bride will find a heavily boned bodice will sit too high.

The Waist:

Notice if the bride has a short waist or has a long waist, the short waist may need letting out at the upper hip if the gown is wrinkling at the waistline or as above the bust area is 'sitting under her chin'.

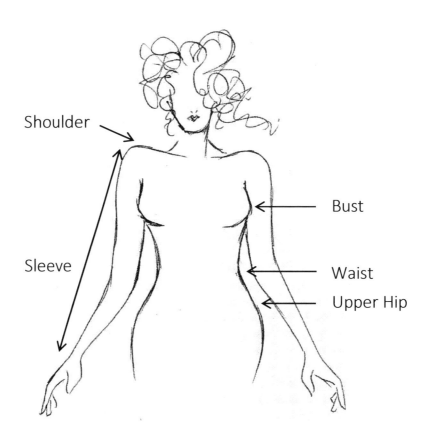

The Upper Hip:

This alteration is used for gowns that have a dropped waist, for sheath or fishtail style gowns where there is no seam around the waistline. The upper hip is an overlooked focal point on bridal gowns. A 'sway back' bride or 'hollow back' cannot have too much taken in at the side seams as this will cause diagonal wrinkles over the lower back thus a centre back alteration will be needed.

Shoulder Lifts:

The majority of bridal gowns will need a small modification done to the shoulder seams. It is important to pin accurately for these, most people will have one shoulder lower than the other.

The principle of altering both sides equally in this instance does not apply.

The Sleeve:

The three areas of adjusting sleeves are:

- *Sleeve head* - Depending on whether a shoulder lift is needed will determine whether the sleeve head will need setting lower, in this instance the entire sleeve may need to be removed. If only a fraction has been taken up then it is possible to 'ease' the head back into position. Gathered sleeves can usually accommodate the extra fullness without too much difficulty.

- *Sleeve width:* pin to the comfort of the bride but remember that arms bend so not too tight.

- *Sleeve cuff:* - if the sleeve cuff has details such as buttons and loops then these will need to be re-positioned and remember that if the sleeve is to be shortened then the width at the wrist will need to be adjusted to accommodate the narrower cuff.

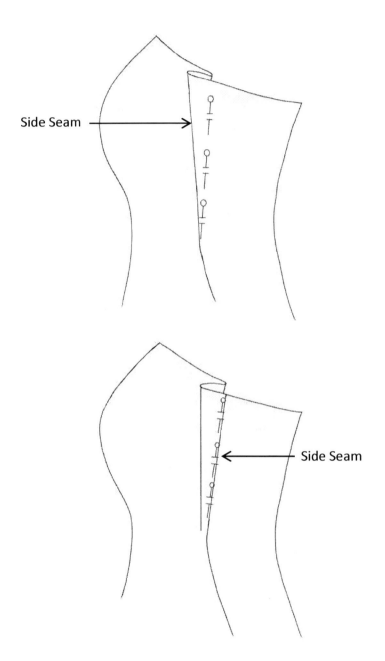

Basic Side Seam:

During the fitting you will notice the gown can be gently pulled at the centre back leaving a smooth fit to the bust area. This means that any excess can be taken in comfortably from both the front and back side seams.

Here the side seam is pinched and pinned where the bodice is loose, taking equal fullness from both the front side seam and the back whilst ensuring the seam itself remains almost vertical without any undue sloping.

This fitting is for brides whose bust cup size is a C but their bust measurement is slightly smaller than the manufacturer's size chart but their waist measurements conform. Bridal weight loss will inevitably lead to taking in slightly on the waistline too. This fitting also works for B cup sizes with the addition of bust cups.

Front Seam:

During the fitting you will notice the gown fits comfortably at the back but sits slightly forward. Fullness is taken from the front side seam. Here the side seam will need to be unpicked and the excess take from the front panel only.

A small amount of excess can also be taken from the back as a combination using the basic side seam and front seam if the bride has a fuller tummy area, but smaller cup size.

It is also possible to add a dart at the side seam to bring the front bodice closer to the body if bringing the side front seam will distort the line of the side seam too much.

This fitting works for A cup sizes and brides with a larger back, this alteration may need couture cups added to fill out the princess seam.

A little help from 'Couture Cups' can be used to fill in the gap and still retain the shape of the princess seam.

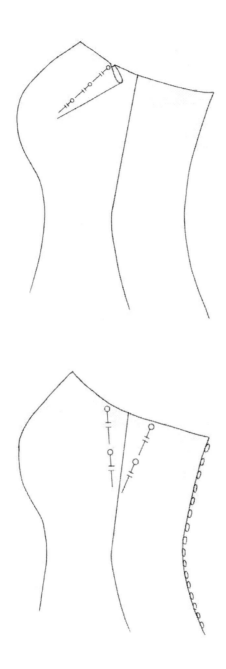

Bust Darts:

A fuller bust will push the bodice away from the body at the upper edge but still fit across the fullest point.

Here the gown is given an extra cup size by adding a dart to the side front panel, allowing the upper edge of the bodice to sit closer to the chest area.

A number of gowns have embellishments such as appliqued lace and sometimes pleating detail, these features are an excellent way of disguising a dart here.

Bust darts that finish at the side seam are useful to add to gowns where the tummy area pushes the bodice away from the body. These are used in conjunction with a front/side seam alteration where the side seam needs to be brought back even further.

Reminder Pins:

Sometimes the fit of the gown is very close or there may be boning restricting the pinch and pin fitting process.

Here 'reminder pins' are useful. They mark the area in need of adjustment.

Notice how on all of the fittings the pins are pointed downwards? This helps to minimise injury during the adjustments.

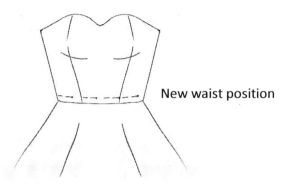

Raising the waist line for a petite bride

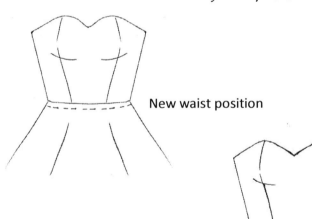

Lengthening the waist line for the tall bride

The Petite & the Tall Bride

The majority of bridal gowns are usually designed to fit a 5ft 8 inch woman. Normally proportion wise this poses few problems and heels are generally worn meaning hemlines need a slight shortening and perhaps the odd shoulder lift.

For dainty brides who are 5ft 3 inches or under then other considerations are needed, proportions will alter the fit of the bodice as well as the length of the skirt.

Common problems occur when the bride's bust, waist and hips measurements match the size chart and the dress will fasten but the bust area will sit practically under the bride's chin.

Sheath style gowns can easily be let out on the upper hip and the waist re-shaped. Gowns with waist seams where the waist line is defined will need the bodice shortened.

To fit this gown unfasten and move the bodice down to fit the bust area. (This can be refined if necessary once the bodice is in the correct position.)

With the gown unfastened have the bride place her hands on her natural waistline. You will notice the slight variation of where the waist of the gown sits in comparison to the bride's waist.

Measure the distance from the waist seam to where the bride's hands denote her waist position. You may wish to mark a line of pins encircling the new waist line.

The dress can now have the skirt removed (the zipper fastening can be unpicked from the skirt with the bodice section remaining in tacked.) The skirt and the lining can be lifted into the new waist position and the lower part of the zipper re-stitched ready for the next fitting.

In contrast taller brides may find the bodice is not quite long enough. Gowns with waist seams can be a little challenging and may require the insertion of a 'belt' to extend the bodice.

This is a common alteration used to lengthen flower girls dresses following a growth spurt. The use of clever applique or belts can be used to disguise any adjustments made. Remember to add length to the lining.

Fitting Hems

The basic principles of fitting wedding dress hems are quite straight forward – in theory. There are however a number of aspects to observe to when the subject of bridal hems comes into focus. For example before a wedding dress hem can be pinned a number of other factors are needed.

- The bodice will need to be adequately adjusted.
- The bride must be wearing any hooped underskirts required.
- The bride must be wearing the shoes she plans on wearing on the day.

When the above have been taken into consideration then the subject of fitting and adjusting the bridal hem can begin.

The Basic Structure of Bridal Skirts

As fashions change so do bridal gowns. Hem length rise and fall and the widths of wedding dresses ebb and flow like the tide of ivory bridal fabrics fall into drapery and sways.

In essence there are a myriad of styles for the bridal attire to take on. The important factor for many manufactured gowns is that they will all conform to a basic shape, whether this is the outer layer or the foundation shape beneath.

Even the most complex of draped skirts will have an underskirt of either an A line, a circular or panelled skirt of any description to support it. It is this foundation that best serves the hemline.

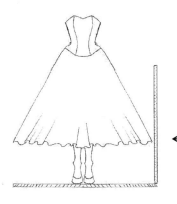

← Use a ruler to mark the position of the hem correctly all the way around.

Full Skirted Gowns

Full skirted gowns come in all shapes, sizes, colours and fabrics, these can vary from countless layers of tulle, draped taffeta, luxurious lace, sumptuous satins and list can go on.

Basically if the fullness of the skirt begins from the upper hip or waist line of the gown and continues in a diagonal direction to the floor with net underskirts it is classed as full skirted.

Circular skirted or 'A' line will also fall into this category. The ideal length for all of these hems would be to skim the floor. The bride should have the illusion of gliding whilst she is walking

Lace Edged Gowns

Lace is used on a great many bridal gowns from the simple sheath dresses to full 'A' line and gorgeous fishtail dresses. As lace gowns will usually be finished with a scalloped edge of hemming lace, these gowns will need the hem to sit with the lower edge of the scallop slightly touching the floor. This will mean that the foundation layer usually satin will need to finish shorter with the hem of the foundation layer level with the apex of the scallop.

This fitting is used for all lace edged hems whether the style is supported by copious amounts of net underskirts or a simple structured gown.

Tea Length & Ballerina Length

These hemlines will require a metre ruler in order to perfect the length. Moving around the bride holding the ruler and pinning as you go will offer the best and level hem needed for these gowns especially if the gown has layers of net underskirts.

Traditionally Tea Length dresses should be mid-calf and ballerina length should sit just above the ankle bone. As with all aspects of fitting bridal gowns there is an element of personal preference and proportion.

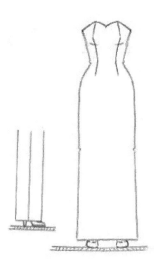

Straight or Column Style Dresses

These gowns have a very structured appearance and are usually created from firm fabrics such as heavy duchesse satin or damask.

Slender gowns will not normally have a train unless it is detachable so the hem must reflect the limitations of the design. The hem should be fitted straight across skimming the tops of the shoes.

As column gowns will have very little shape to the side seams the gown must remain as straight as possible, curving the hem to allow it to flow longer at the back will form too many creases and distort the overall style.

Chiffon & other soft flowing fabrics

For the slender, willowy gown fabrics that have more of fluidity are used. Fabrics such as chiffon and crepe have body conscious styles.

For these hems the foundation layer will sit approximately 1.5 – 2cms shorter than the actual fashion layer, the outer layer will simply skim the floor. When the bride walks the tips of her shoes should be visible.

Slender gowns without netting will usually have the lining anchored to the C/B seam and will therefore move with the train. This lining should be shorter than the fashion fabric by approximately 1.5 – 2cms.

As with all gowns recommend the best fitting line but be mindful of what your customer wishes, some brides like to have the hem touching the floor.

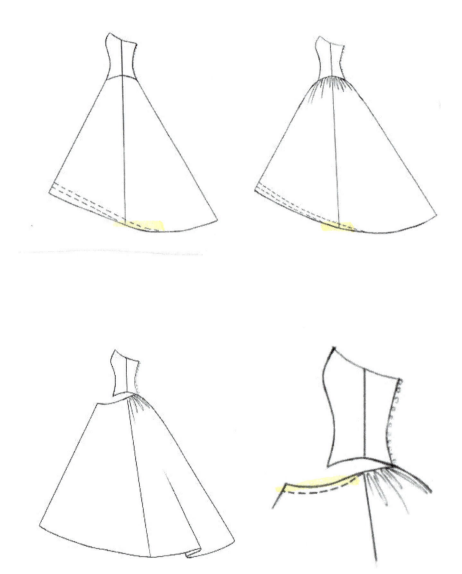

The Basic Hem Fitting

Even novice dressmakers will understand the principles of how to turn up a hem, whether it is for a pair of jeans that are too long or a skirt that needs re-modelling to make a more fashionable length it is simply a case of folding up the excess and pinning.

Bridal gowns are not too dissimilar. These basic diagrams are demonstrating where the new hemline would be sitting. The upper broken line denotes the position for a petite bride, notice how the new hem will continue past the side seams?

Shortening From the Waist

Bridal gowns can also be adjusted from the waistline. This type of alteration is used for heavily detailed gowns that have embellishments to the hem such as embroidery that cannot be removed.

The fitting will be undertaken in the traditional way with the hem turned up from the lower edge, but the alteration itself is performed at the waist seam.

Here the waistline of the gown is unpicked to just past the side seams. A note is made of the amount the hem has been turned up by and this measurement will then be removed from the waist seam on the skirt, this will start from the C/F and grade out to the side seam in a smooth line.

If the bride is petite then more will need trimming slightly beyond the side seam of the skirt to ensure a smooth grading of the waist seam.

As the gown has a gathered skirt the added width of skirt can be easily absorbed into the gathers.

Fitting Figures

With so many figure shapes and sizes it is nigh impossible to consider all the possibilities. Combine this with the infinite combinations of styles, fabrics, and finishes and we seamstresses really do have our work cut out for us.

In this chapter I'll take you through a number of scenarios and where you can expect to make alterations.

Remember that for each figure there will be variations such as cup sizes and personal preference such as heel heights, or more cleavage, some brides prefer comfort other may prefer style.

Always ask your bride, as a dressmaker you are there also to offer your expert advice as well as your services, your role is not all about sewing.

For the purposes of this chapter I will be using the same style gown to illustrate the various options for the various figure shapes. Once again these are just a few of the combinations of figure and dress you may come across.

The illustration opposite is the stylised image a bride may wish to emulate for the fishtail or mermaid style gown.

I have included working drawings for both the front and the back to display the seamlines and structure along with a brief description of the type of fabrics that would be used for this style of gown.

The Dress Basics:

A classic fishtail style gown with a waved neckline on a bustier based bodice. An upper bodice with high neck and full length fitted sleeves made of tulle is fitted to the lower bodice bustier. This is sometimes referred to as an illusion neckline.

The gown has a base fabric of heavy duchesse satin; this is 'bagged out' with lining fabric sometimes called 'clean finished' essentially the satin is fully lined throughout. The satin is overlaid with tulle and this has beaded lace applique mirror imaged throughout the gown, including the neckline and sleeves.

The hem is finished with a beaded edging lace with a slight scallop.

A full length lining is fitted to the gown and this is boned using the manufactured method, with one layer of netting stitched at knee level creating the fullness at the hem.

The gown is fastened with a standard zipper at the centre back finishing at the upper edge of the bustier, the illusion upper bodice is fastened by elasticated loops and covered buttons both at the centre back and the cuffs. As the illusion neckline is not under strain the loops do not need to be replaced with handmade rouleaux loops. Covered buttons are stitched for decoration only on the lower bodice.

Bridal Sizing

Bridal sizes are very different to standard high street sizes and on the whole tend to be on the slightly smaller size. For example a bridal size 12 would measure up to bust: 36 C, waist: 27, low hip: 38 and sizes normally go up by 2 inches.

Gowns are generally designed to fit a woman of 5ft 8" wearing two inch heels.

Anything more than a size 18 is considered to be a plus size. This is the limit of the standard block, after this size the proportions and curves tend to alter slightly.

Sadly many plus sizes offered have not been thoughtfully graded, yes the manufacturer can offer them but all they have done is continue to grade up from size 12 blocks.

Curvy brides are just that, and as such need a specific block that starts from size 18 measurement but conforms to slightly different contours.

There are a few companies who have understood this and altered their collection accordingly, but for the majority of manufactured gowns brides are stuck with a dress that really doesn't conform to their curves at all.

This is where us dressmakers come into the dressing room and wave our magic pin cushion.

Petite sizes will be graded differently too, for example the nape to waist will be shorter as will the hem lengths and sleeve lengths.

Many bridal manufacturers do not do a petite range as this is a whole different block that would need to be created so it would not be cost effective for them.

Again here are a few specialist companies who manufacturer the specific petite range but not too many.

Scenario 1 – The Hourglass

Height: 5ft 7"

Heel height: 3 "

Bust: 36 C

Waist: 26"

Hips: 36"

Bridal size: 12

Okay we'll start with an easy one. The bride in this instance has needed to have a size 12 gown ordered based on her bust measurement.

The Bodice:

Proportion wise she is 5ft 7" and she will be wearing 3 inch heels so the nape to waist will sit very well, the sleeve length and skirt length will be perfect.

The gown is heavily boned in the bodice with a good support around the back so this bride should have no issues when it comes to the bust position and she is a cup size C so this will be sitting comfortably.

The upper bodice should be fitting well but I would check on the shoulders as most people will have one shoulder lower than the other and this may affect the fit slightly and cause sagging on one side.

This alteration will involve the removal of one or both sleeves in order to adjust the shoulder seams – quite a big job for just one small alteration.

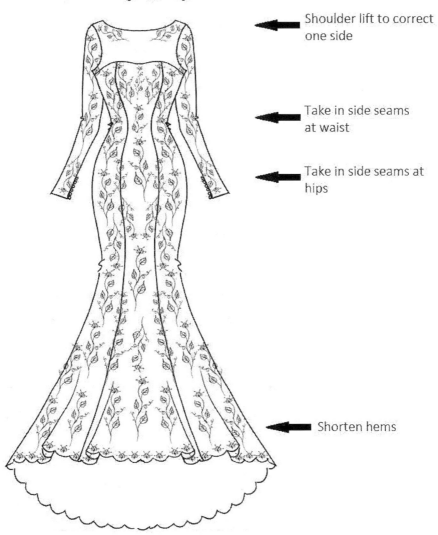

The Skirt:

The gown is a size 12 so the waist measurement will be a little loose as will the hips.

Both these areas can be to be taken in at the side seams. For this I would check that the side seams have been manufactured using the 'combination seams' method, this will help with the alteration considerably.

If the tulle layer is stitched separately then I will created a combined seam for the purpose of the alteration. (See the Chapter on *Combined Seams* it will help enormously when undertaking bridal alterations.)

I will need to ensure that any beaded applique is removed, retained and once the fitting is complete re-stitched if necessary. Sometimes appliqué straddles over seams, usually over princess seams to disguise or simply as part of a design feature.

Finally to complete this alteration I would fit Victorian bustle tapes to the centre back and the two back princess seams.

As this gown is made from heavy duchesse satin, bagged out and is embellished with a beaded tulle over overlay this will be incredibly heavy, so this requires a more substantial bustle one that will not damage the dress.

With all bridal fittings the bride must have a few lessons on how to behave like a bride.

She and her bridal party must be instructed on how to get into the dress, how to walk, how to stand, how to sit down and kneel.

Then there are the lessons on how to create the Victorian bustle. I very often give out a card to my brides; it is almost like their homework, because after all it isn't every day a wedding dress is worn.

The Apple Shaped Figure

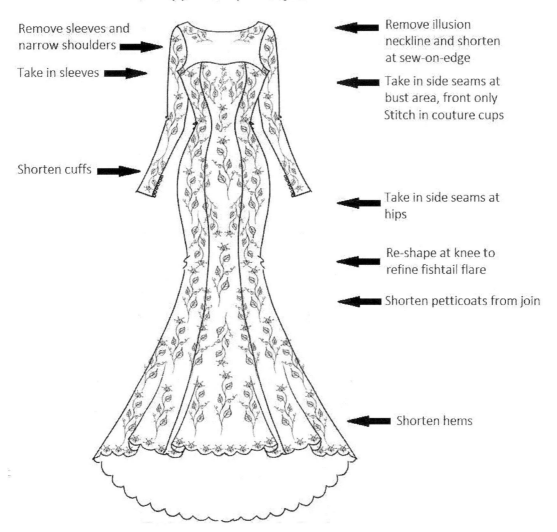

- Remove sleeves and narrow shoulders
- Take in sleeves
- Shorten cuffs
- Remove illusion neckline and shorten at sew-on-edge
- Take in side seams at bust area, front only Stitch in couture cups
- Take in side seams at hips
- Re-shape at knee to refine fishtail flare
- Shorten petticoats from join
- Shorten hems

Scenario 2 – The Apple Shape

Height: 5ft 5"

Heel height: 2 "

Bust: 38 B

Waist: 37"

Hips: 36"

Bridal size: 22

This brides figure conforms to the apple shape. The gown size would be based on the waist measurement which is significantly larger than the hips.

At 5ft 5" she is of average height so technically the nape to waist would be a reasonable fit, but due to bridal sizes of 22 the grading aspect would increase this.

The Bodice,

The bodice would need to be taken in at the side seams from the front to sit closer to the chest as the tummy area would be pushing the bodice out slightly.

The bride is a B cup so will need couture cups stitched to fill out the bust area; a bust dart from the side seam may also be needed to level the neckline and bring the bustier closer to the body.

Apple shapes (and straight figure shapes) may have very little curve at lower back so the centre back may need taking in too.

This will involve unpicking the zipper from below the waist and taking in the centre back seam.

Upper bodice:

The illusion neckline will need to be completely adjusted, the most effective way would be to separate it from the main gown and work on it as a separate piece. It can be shortened at the sew-on-edge thus the shoulders would not need to be taken up and the neckline will remain the correct shape.

This sounds complicated but by separating the upper bodice from the main gown you are able to work on individual sections of the dress much more effectively and are less likely to do any damage whilst working.

The shoulders may need to be narrowed so the sleeves will have to be removed. The sleeves will need to be taken in and possibly shortened. This will require the applique along with the buttons and loops removed and put back. Alternatively the sleeve head can be re-shaped and the reduction can be taken from the top.

The Skirt

Here the side seams will need attention over the lower hip area. With a tulle/lace overlay the side seams could well be constructed using the *'combination seams'* method. If not then this would be the opportunity to create them, check if the applique will hinder the alteration if so remove and re-apply following the fitting.

The Hems;

At 5ft 5" and with only 2 inch heels the front hem will need to be adjusted, grading it back into the side seams. This will involve shortening the satin underskirt and lifting the lace edging.

The petticoat will only need to be adjusted where the netting is stitched to the lining.

To finish as before Victorian bustle tapes can be stitched into the skirt.

Scenario 3 – The Straight Figure Shape

Height: 5ft 7"

Heel height: flat"

Bust: 32 A

Waist: 28"

Hips: 34"

Bridal size: 12

On first analysis this bride's measurement could well fall into the apple or the pair shape, but this bride has a straight figure type.

She has a dainty cup size and her hip measurement is only 6" larger than her waist, she is perhaps naturally willowy or enjoys running as an exercise. As size charts go she crosses several sizes, bust 32 A would put her at a size 8, her waist puts her between a size 12 and 14 but her hips offer up a size 10.

There is normally a little bit of ease with most gowns and a good bit of seam allowance. For the sake of 1 inch the shop would have ordered a size 12. A size 14 would totally swamp her delicate frame and would cause major downsizing issues.

At 5ft 7" proportion wise the bust, waist, hips and the nape to waist will all sit in the correct position. There may be a slight shoulder adjustment needed as most people have one lower than the other, *I blame shoulder bags and years of carrying them*.

The Upper Bodice

Once again the upper bodice will need attention. The illusion neckline may not need to be completely removed; the centre front and centre back can stay attached if preferred.

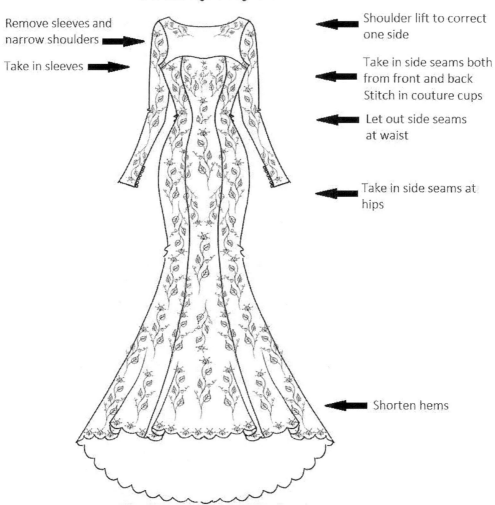

The shoulders will need to be narrowed so there is the removal of the sleeves and these will also need to be taken in. This will require the loops and buttons removing and re-attached. The sleeve length should be the correct, *so that is one less job to do!*

The Bodice:

Brides do tend to lose weight so by the time the day of the fitting arrives the dress should zip up and have very few issues around the waist area. Failing this then the side seams can be let out a fraction at the waistline. Again check for the combination seams as this will make the following alterations run far more smoothly.

The bust area will need to be taken in at the sides seams equal amounts from the front and the back. Foam couture cups will be needed to fill the gap between the princess seams and the body.

This bride has narrow hips so the side seams will need to be taken in, again as before the 'combination seams' will aid the alteration.

The Hem:

Finally as the bride favours flat shoes the hem will need to be shortened slightly.

By slightly this does not imply that the alteration will take any less time. The same procedures will still apply whether it is by 2 inches or 6. The satin will need shortening and the edging lace removed, lifted and hand stitched back into place.

To complete the alterations a Victorian bustle tapes.

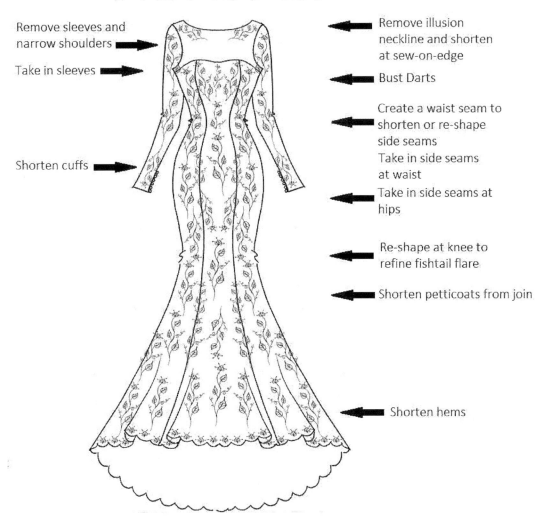

Scenario 4 – The Petite Pair Shape

Height: 5ft 1"

Heel height: 4 "

Bust: 34 D

Waist: 25"

Hips: 36"

Bridal size: 10

For this example the bride's measurements put her at a manufacturer's size 10. Her cup size of D will mean the gown fits quite snugly across her chest and will need a bust dart to keep the bodice sitting close over her bosom.

At 5ft 1" the gown is going to be too long in the nape to waist, waist to floor and in the sleeves. A common issue for petite brides or short-waisted women although their bust waist and hip measurements conform to any given size chart the problems usually present themselves on the waist area.

Bridal gowns highlight this issue due to the profuse amount of boning that hold the shape of the bodice. When the gown is fastened the bust area is forced to sit incredibly high. Gowns with less boning will simply wrinkle around the waist, usually more noticeable at the back.

For this alteration there is a considerable amount of fitting needed. To begin with I would concentrate on the waist and bust; by redefining the waist area the bust shaping will conform better. There are two methods of dealing with the shortening of the waist:

1. The side seams can be let out below the bride's natural waistline and taken in just above. This will shunt the whole bodice area slightly lower and allow the bust position to sit correctly and not somewhere under her chin.

2. If there is insufficient seam allowance then a waist seam can be created. This will work well on this dress as there is an abundance of applique that can be used to disguise the seam.

Many dresses can be adjusted in this way if there is applique or pleating to be taken advantage of, plain dresses may need the addition of a belt to conceal it.

This 2nd alternative will involve removing the zipper part way and unpicking the boning from the waist down in order to make the seam. The boning and the zipper can be re-attached in their new positions.

Whilst working on the bodice the waist can also be taken in at the same time. And possibly the hips, again the 'combined seams' method will be truly invaluable for this bride and her alterations.

The Upper Bodice

1. The upper bodice is shortened at the sew-on-edge of the neckline. This, although sounds complicated it will simplify a number of other modifications that will also be needed (see 2nd option) as mentioned the gown will need bust darts.

So by removing the illusion neckline this alteration will be easier to perform as two procedures can be undertaken with far more ease.

2. The second option involves much more work and is very restricting due to the volume of dress that will need to be manoeuvred. A shoulder lift will need the removal of the sleeves, lowering of the neckline including the unpicking of the applique.

The illusion sew-on-edge will also need to be taken in under the arm in order to accommodate the bust dart.

Quite simply the dress is in need of re-making so the best and most cost effective way is to strip it back to separate parts and work on them individually.

Sleeves:

Whilst the illusion neckline is a separate piece it will be easier to work on the sleeves, these will need removing and the shoulders narrowed. The sleeves will also need to be taken in slightly and this will continue under the arm hole to the short side seam where it joins the main bodice.

The cuffs will also require shortening this will involve removing the beaded applique along with the loops and buttons. As the cuff will become wider the higher up the sleeve then the sleeve will also need to be taken in slightly to accommodate the new position of the cuff. Or as before the sleeve head can be reduced.

Re-shaping the Fishtail Skirt

This is perhaps one aspect that is overlooked on quite a few petite brides and their alterations.

Most will assume that the shape of the skirt is perfectly acceptable and will need no further alterations. However the fishtail element will need refining slightly.

If you imagine the flare of the fishtail will usually occur near to the knee area, on our petite bride her knees will be lower to the ground, even by lifting from the waist the flare aspect will still be sitting too low.

For this alteration the side seams will need to be unpicked at the mid-thigh down to the calf and the 'flare' re-introduced a little higher. This will correct all the proportions.

Shortening the Hems

This will involve four procedures possibly five. The first is where the netting is joined to the lining will need to be shortened; this will keep the proportion of the netting to knee length where it is needed to hold out the skirt, remember we discussed the re-shaping of the fishtail skirt above.

The petticoat will need to be shortened at the hem all the way around ensuring that it is floor length and no train remains.

Experience has taught me that these only serve to trip up the bride; a train is only needed on the fashion fabric and should only be lined if it is either bagged out or anchored near to the hem. Lining petticoats that support the netting do not need trains.

As the bride is very petite the netting may be shortened at the hem also. If the netting has a finish such as lace edging or crin/horsehair then remove and re-attach.

The foundation skirt made of satin has a bagged out lining, here the hem will need to be unpicked at the front and part way around past the side seams this will ensure the skirt hem has a smooth transition back into the train.

Finally, the beaded lace hem can be shortened. The appliqued lace edging will have to be removed, raised and hand stitched back into position.

So to finish the gown will also need several pairs Victorian bustle tapes.

***

Perhaps not the most straight-forward of alterations but this one does represent the amount of work that can be required; thankfully most dresses will not need quite such a major overhaul.

This chapter has highlighted quite a number of scenarios when it comes to figure types and the adjustments that can be made.

Just by using one style of gown as an example we have seen how it can be fitted and adjusted to suit four very different figures, from the barely anything to a complete re-make of the gown.

The Inner workings of a Wedding Dress

The bridal gown has become a fairy-tale affair, a mysterious magical item of clothing worn by those who cherish love and romance.

For those of us who work in the bridal industry we see wedding dresses somewhat differently especially us dressmakers.

Seamstresses view a wedding dress as a thing of great workmanship, we enthuse over the finer details of beadwork design, bugle beads and pearls are an endless source of fascination to us.

We love nothing more than to get up close and personal with a bridal gown and examine the seams that have been used, measure the seam allowances and marvel at the delicate nature of a French seam on chiffon.

Bridal gowns have that romance that harks back to history, to a time where fair maidens were rescued by the hansom price who swept them up onto a white steed wrapping a strong arm around a slender waist... *okay I'm getting carried away here.*

Therein is the eternal secret and infinite charm of a wedding dress. Every princess would have had a tiny waist formed by an un-yielding contraption – the boned corset.

Boning is the mainstay of many bridal gowns and the ways of stitching it into dress are numerous.

These final chapters will be covering just a few of the most popular 'inner workings' of a bridal gown the essential and inspiring ways the gorgeous dresses we work on are put together.

The Boned Bodice

Re-Stitching the Boning

When it comes to adjusting bridal gowns the main alteration points for bodices are the side seams. But when it comes to altering a bridal gown most novice seamstresses will balk at the very idea of removing boning simply on the principle that it cannot be stitched back into the original position.

Manufacturers labour intensively on achieving the perfect bust seam so unless the alteration involves downsizing by more than 6 inches/15 cms then the side seams offer the perfect opportunity to fit a gown This ensures that the bust, waist and hip ratio are maintained.

Boning fitted to or near the side seams comes in a variety of formats, when altering bridal gowns knowing the diverse ways of how it can be re-applied once all of the alterations have been undertaken will help to achieve a perfect finished look to the dress.

The most frequently used boning used in bridal wear both in the mass produced method and the couture bodice is the polyester tubular variety and the widths used can vary. It is lightweight, easy to use, and inexpensive.

The most important factor when working with boning is to ensure the ends are capped. For the polyester tubular boning this is simply a case of folding over and stitching a piece of scrap fabric on each end. This prevents any of the filaments from causing injury to the wearer and must be done on every piece of boning used.

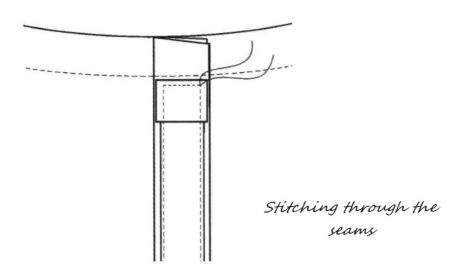

Stitching through the seams

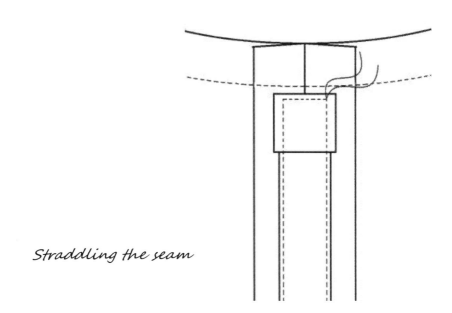

Straddling the seam

Stitching Through Seams:

Here the seam is pressed to one side and the boning is stitched in line with the seam through all of the layers with the stitching visible on the right side. This is commonly seen on princess seams both front and back.

You will also notice when you work with bridal gowns that the front princess seams can either be pressed open or pressed to the middle. This is the choice of the manufacturer, and again there is no better or preferred method.

Princess seams will usually carry the 7mm width boning, whilst for the side seams it will be the sturdier 12mm width.

Straddling The Seam

Here the boning is positioned straddling the pressed open seam and stitched though. This is used either for princess seams or side seams.

As with all manufactured gowns both of these techniques are stitched at the beginning of production; to re-apply the boning in this way then the gown would need to be taken apart in order to access the seams from the correct side.

There are however alternative ways of applying boning to bodices and these are useful when altering gowns.

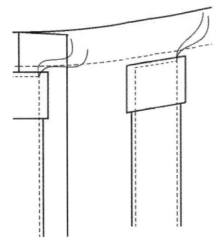
Directly stitched boning

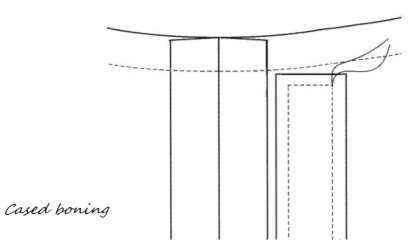
Cased boning

Directly Stitched Boning

Directly stitched boning is used widely, it does not follow seam lines rather it sits between them. This is commonly found down the centre front between the princess seams to add a 'busk'* effect to the bodice.

It can also be stitched throughout the bodice where ever the designer or manufacturer decides to place it.

If a side seam needs taking in and there is the directly stitched boning running alongside, then usually this can be removed without the need for it to be re-attached. Generally there will be insufficient space due to the adjustment.

**A Busk was a rod of wood, bone or metal inserted into the centre front of corsets or 'stays' to keep the front ridged and straight.*

Cased Boning

The cased boning is often seen in bridesmaid gowns and uses the hard plastic variety.

Here a piece of bias lining fabric cut slightly wider than the actual boning is stitched directly onto the bodice lining usually running alongside the side seams. The boning is inserted into the casing and secured.

During the alteration process the side seams will need to be unpicked in order to re-site the bias casing and the boning.

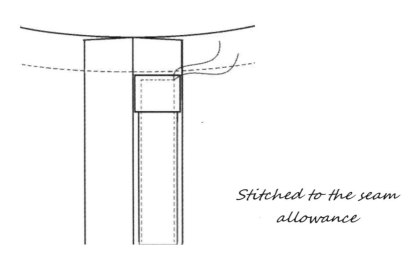

Stitched to the seam allowance

Stitched To The Seam Allowance

This works well for side seams where there is too much bulk to fit under your machine. The boning is only stitched to the seam allowance not directly through to the right side. When the garment is worn the boning will sit flat against the body.*

This technique can also be used for the canvas bodices where the side seams are constructed by straddling the seam. Attaching the boning in this way can be tricky so tacking it into position or even hand sewing may prove worthwhile.

*Boned side seams are quite common, they can however prove problematic. Side seams should only be boned if the gown has a waist seam, this can be high, natural position or high hip.

Side seam boning should be avoided on slim fitting sheath or fishtail gowns. Primarily there is no natural 'cut off' point for the boning so it will jut out from the hip or jab into the waist. It is better removed altogether.

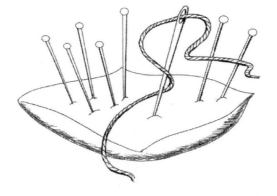

Combination Seams

This type of seam as with most sewing skills will have multiple names; this is what I call it. I have asked many professional dressmaker friends of mine and they are all in agreement, they have no idea of its technical name either.

These are quite unusual seams as they combine two or more layers of fabric into one seam, this seam is then snipped and the upper layers of fabric are left to glide or float over the foundation layer.

It is a manufacturing technique that works incredibly well for alteration purposes.

This seam involves one or more layers of delicate fabric such as lace, chiffon, tulle or organza that will be overlaid over a base fabric for example satin.

This type of seam is a fantastic way of combining multiple layers of fabric to give a smooth and accurate seam, allowing for a better fit and ease of alteration.

The process itself is quite straightforward, once you understand how the process works. Many wedding dress alterations that seem initially complicated or time consuming will be quite stress-free once you understand the production techniques used and how it can be adapted for a more successful alteration.

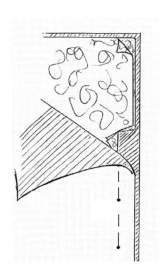
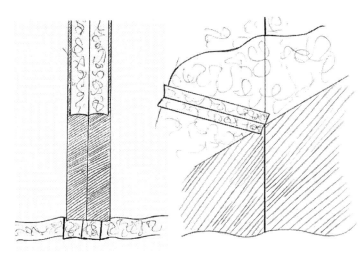

The overlay is first stitched below the notch, the seam can be pressed open in the case of lace or organza or chiffon may be French seamed so will be pressed to the back.

The notch/snip should make a right angle and the notch must be close enough to the seam. The overlay is sandwiched between the foundation layers (for example satin).

Notice the seamed part of the lace has been folded out of the way below the notch? This is to allow the seam to be completed and the floating layer will not be caught up in the foundation layer seam.

The overlay and the foundation layer can be stitched as one seam from the top down to the snipped area with the foundation layer finished in a continual seam.

This can now be pressed open or overlocked depending on the fabric and the finish required. The illustration shows the internal seams pressed open and the continual line of the satin or foundation layer.

Combination seam overlays can be fitted in any number of ways, some stop at the upper hip some continue the full length of the side seam to within a few cms of the hems. The second lower diagram shows the completed seam with the overlay lifted.

This method of seaming multiple layers of fabric can be adapted to other gowns that have a tricky side seams to alter especially in the bodice area.

They are also useful for fish tale gowns where multiple layers of tulle are also tricky to take in individually. These seams extend the area of the side seam offering a better fit and flair.

It is worth noting that letting out this style of seam can only be done to the notch position due to the snipped seam.

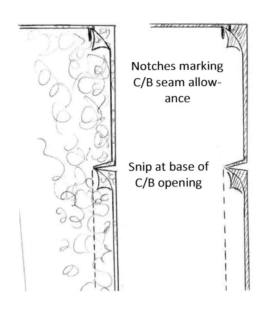

Notches marking C/B seam allowance

Snip at base of C/B opening

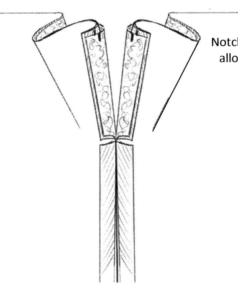

Notches marking C/B seam allowance on each layer

A variation of this technique can also be used for centre back openings.

Where a lightweight overlay is used such as organza, lace, tulle, chiffon etc. a similar method can be employed for the insertion of zippers, buttons or to create a lattice back gown. This essentially creates one firm seam instead of several delicate seams.

The overlay is snipped to correspond with the foundation layer and as before the seam is stitched below the notch.

The overlay seams are finished appropriate to the nature of the fabric for example chiffon and organza would be French seamed, lace and tulle would be left unfinished and pressed open.

The foundation layer (for example satin) would be usually pressed open; if the gown was 'bagged out' then the seams would not need to be overlocked to prevent fraying.

Next, the wrong side of the overlay is placed onto the right side of the foundation layer matched to the notched part of the seam.

The snipped upper layer is then wrapped around the foundation layer. The two layers of fabric can then be stitched around the open part of the seam to secure.

The opening can be worked with much more easily when it comes to inserting a zipper, creating a button stand with loops or lattice back corset.

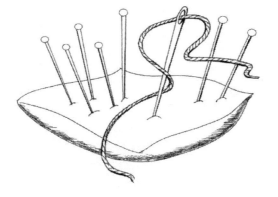

Bindings

Bias binding has various uses in general sewing and clothing production. In manufactured bridal gowns it can be used for hems, necklines, waistlines and armholes used as both a decorative trim and as a finishing for seams.

For traditional bindings these can either be bought pre-folded – where the two long edges are neatly folded ready for stitching or bias binding can be hand cut and using a fun little tool can be folded by using an iron. Or whilst you're sewing a special foot can be clipped onto your machine.

Binding can be finished in two ways, with top stitching through all of the layers or one edge of the binding machined into place with the opposite side then slip stitched on the reverse.

In manufacturing hand stitching would be too time-consuming so factories use the *stitch- in-the- ditch* method or *sink stitching*.

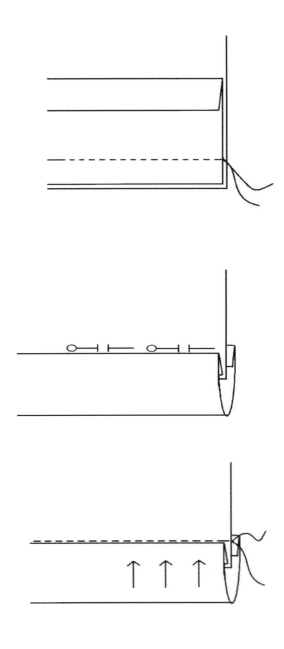

Mock Hand Stitched Binding

For this method the seam allowance on one side of the binding is first pressed, and then the un-pressed side of the binding is stitched along the raw edge for example on a hem.

For hand finishing the binding is folded over to enclose the raw edges. The 2nd fold of binding would sit level with the first and would be either slip stitched or top stitched through.

In manufacturing this edge is eased very slightly to sit approx. 1-2mm past the first fold – this is more noticeable on fine fabrics such as chiffon or organza

The 2nd row of stitching is then stitched close to the fold of the first – sink stitched.

Finally the binding is rolled and pressed to cover the 2nd row of stitching this creates a very slight tuck on the right side of the fabric.

The binding now looks hand finished with an absence of visible stitching.

These bound edges come in all widths from the very narrow to finish necklines and armholes to a deep edging with a finished width of 5 – 6 cms to edge hemlines

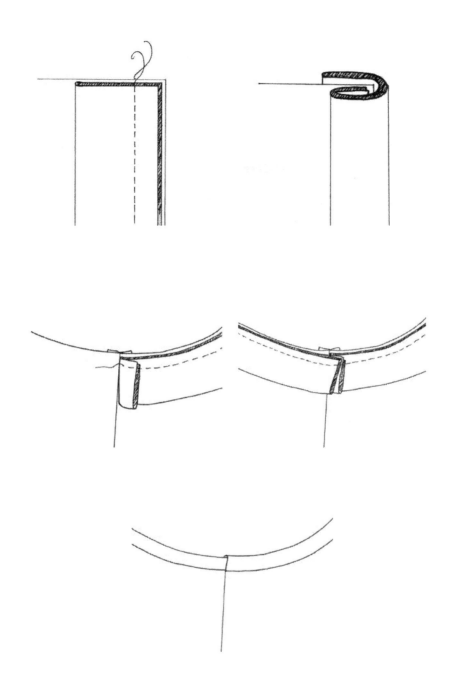

Double Folded Bindings

For fuller seams that need a bound edge such as sleeve armholes or sometimes waistlines then a much wider bias strip is cut. This time the binding is folded in half length-ways down the centre.

For this technique the binding will be need to be 6 x the width of the seam allowance. Due to the bulk this finishing process favours using light weight fabric such as organza or tulle or a light weight satin can be used.

If the binding is a woven fabric then it will be cut on the bias, if the fabric is tulle for example a knitted fabric then it will be cut with the knit offering the most stretch so across the fabric and not down – imagine a welt on a sweat shirt.

The raw edge of the binding rests along the raw edge of the armhole; this is placed on the bodice side.

Begin from the side seam and fold the short edge so it is in line with the seam, pin and tack if necessary before stitching the binding to all the way around the armhole.

When the start position is reached, finish the binding so that it overlaps the fold.

Trim if necessary and fold the binding over the raw edge working the bias with your fingers to mould into the curve.

Pin and tack into position this can either be hand stitched or machine depending on the size of the aperture. In industry this would be machined.

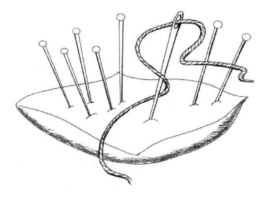

A Bit of Hand Sewing

For most seamstresses the hand sewing element of dressmaking marks the near completion of a garment. In bridal alterations so much time is dedicated to both the unpicking and the finishing with a small operation sandwiched between. Those small details such as French tacks or the stitching of buttons heralds a job well done.

There are no mystifying secrets to hand finishing and most dressmakers will be familiar and have more than enough in their repertoire of needlecraft to complete many a garment.

The following are simply a few commonly used techniques used to finish bridal gowns

Sewing Beads

The most time consuming aspect of any bridal alteration is the un-picking and the finishing off. This is never truer than with beadwork.

In an ideal situation then any loose threads should be pulled through to the reverse and tied off, however many bridal gowns do not have this option.

In some instances the beadwork application is directly onto the fashion fabric and the threads sit between that and the interlining or the beadwork is first stitched to appliquéd pieces such as lace motifs.

The best method of stitching beads back into position is the following:

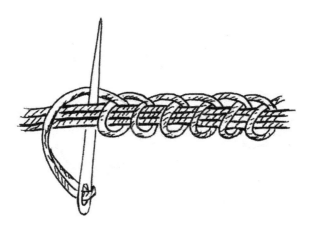

Once all of the alterations are complete take an empty *crewel* needle carefully make a stitch next to the loose thread with the 'eye' parallel to the thread and almost through the fabric.

Trim the thread to 'sharpen' the fibres and insert the ends of the thread through the eye. Continue with the stitch. Repeat this to finish off and trim the thread. Any other beads may now be stitched back into place.

If there is insufficient loops thread available simply follow the thread back to the next bead and remove until there is enough thread to work with.

French Tacks

They are used as belt carriers, button loops, securing multiple layers of fabric near to hem lines, for securing multiple layers near to the bustle position; the use of these are quite endless.

There are two methods of producing these useful little strings of thread; style.

Blanket Stitch French Tack

The most well-known method is the 'blanket stitch' here multiple threads are used to make a double-double threaded needle. Begin by securing to one layer of fabric this is very often on a seam, then passing the needle to the same place on the second layer, leaving a short length of thread approximately 2-3 cms spanning the two pieces.

You can also use strong thread for these you wish. Secure and return back to the original starting point.

There are now multiple threads. Holding the thread in your left hand close to the base of the thread take the needle and thread lay it over the span of threads and bring up between the two.

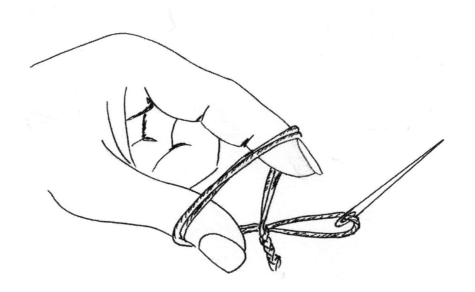

Pull gently to tighten the stitch – imagine the span is the edge of fabric and you are blanket stitching this. Continue all the way along the span keeping the thread taught enough so as not to twist.

When you reach the opposite end, finish off.

Chain Stitch French Tack.

If you are familiar with the technique of crochet then you will see the similarities with this stitch. Begin as before by double-doubling the thread and securing to one side of the fabric. Make another stitch close to your starting point but do not pull the thread tight, this should be big enough to hold your thumb and index finger with a gap between of approximately 3-4 cms.

Hold the thread that carries the needle taught and vertical against the loop sitting between your thumb and finger, use your pincer grip to capture the thread and draw it through the opening, gently pull to tighten the loop.

Repeat this process until the chain stitch is of the required length.

To finish pass the needle through the loop and pull to tighten. The chain thread can now be anchored to the corresponding fabric it needs to join.

This is an incredibly fast and efficient way to produce a French tack, although like most stitching it does need a little practice.

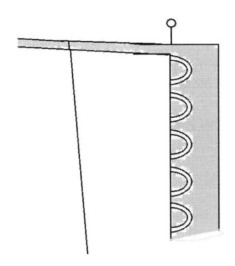
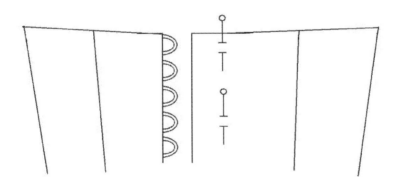

Buttons

A great many bridal gowns will either be fastened using buttons or will use buttons as a design feature.

Should the fitting process involve a centre back alteration then the re-stitching of buttons may be necessary.

The technically minded may be thinking of utilising a ruler to measure the exact positioning of the buttons, however bridal gowns and their subsequent alterations very rarely conform or succumb to such nonsense.

The best technique I have found is to first count how many buttons have been removed and set aside the same number of pins.

For gowns that are fastened using the couture method first lightly fold the dress lengthways and line up the back princess seams to each other, next mark the centre back position on the button stand.

Pin a line equal distance from top to bottom.

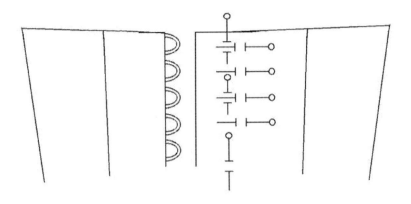
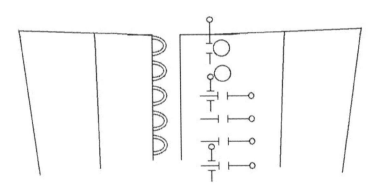

Align the button loop centre back over the button stand and position a pin to correspond where the upper most of the buttons will sit and then its counterpart at the bottom.

The buttons must sit slightly to the right of the centre back. This allows the centre back to align itself and takes into account the pull of the loop when the gown is fastened.

Take the remaining pins and simply fill in the space between, using your eye to measure. Attempting to accurately measure the distance between the buttons will leave a short fall due to the gentle curve of the centre back.

Using a double-double threaded needle begin at the base of the buttons and secure the thread. Work the needle horizontally and thread the needle through button shank in the same way. This allows the tension to be taken by the thread not the shank.

Stitch though twice and finish off on the reverse, but do not snip the thread.

Carefully glide the needle between the layers and emerge where the next button will sit. Repeat this process until all the buttons have been stitched into place.

Design feature buttons can be re-stitched in exactly the same way. First count the number of buttons and loops (this is worth checking just in case an extra one has been added or one is missing) then count out the same number of pins, begin to place them along the seam or centre back position.

Using a double-double threaded needle as before, stitch the buttons into position.

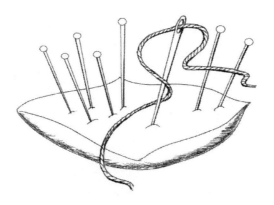

And so, to sew...

I do hope you have enjoyed this little introduction into the world of bridal fittings and alterations.

But there is so much more to discover. For example one of the most sought after skills in the repertoire of a seamstress is the ability to create a corset backed gown.

In bridal shops it could be the make or break of a sale, a bride falls in love with a dress but it's two sizes too small, how about adding a corset back? Sometimes it is due to necessity, the bride has the delightful news she is expecting, perhaps she is a bridesmaid and intends on wearing the dress regardless of the ever growing bump.

Lace edged hems, 'What magic do you perform to keep all of the detail on the hem...?' I was asked by one bride.

'Magic, simply magic oh, and a bit of sewing know how.'

Weddings are a huge investment for individuals and we as dressmakers are in an enviable position to help make dreams come true for the bride and her attendants.

We really do have magic fingers and we have the power to make every bride's wedding a truly fairy-tale event.

If you would like to know more about the bridal industry then I have other titles that may whet your interest.

Would you like to discover more about bridal alterations? Would you like to learn how to make bridal rouleaux loops and how to put a corset back into a gown, what to do with a low décolletage and how to prevent the bride from spilling out? How about creating a Victorian bustle?

Have you ever wanted to open your own bridal shop, but can't sew a button on? Not a problem, no sewing required, you just need the passion for working with gorgeous dresses and helping brides choose the perfect gown for their big day. So please do read on.

Perhaps you have a yearning to launch your own couture bridal label and your own shop selling your wonderful designs to brides?

My books are designed specifically for those wishing to have a career in the bridal industry, whether your passion is retail, design or sewing there will be a book perfect for you.

All that is left is to thank you for reading this book; I hope it has inspired you to venture forward and discover more about the wonderful world of wedding dresses and possibly become part of a unique band of people who help to make dreams come true.

Warmest wishes

Sarah x

Glossary

A
A Line skirt – a skirt shape depicting the form of the letter A.
Applique method of applying decoration to the surface of fabric

B
Bagged out – term used for garments that have the lining attached to the hem, also known as clean finished.
Basting – see tacking stitches
Boat neck – a high neckline that finishes close to the edge of the shoulders.
Body tape- double side, hypoallergenic sticky tape sued to secure garments to the body.
Bustle – the method by which the train of a bridal gown can be lifted up for the evening.

C
Chantilly lace – a lightweight delicate lace produced in France.
Chiffon – diaphanous fabric
Circular skirt – a skirt that has been cut using a full circle to add volume to the hem.
Cinch – an elasticated 'belt' to bring in areas of a bodice to make them appear tighter.
Corded lace – a heavy weight lace using a cord that has been couch stitched into position.
Couture stitching – delicate stitching
Corseting – a method of fastening gowns using cord to tighten.
Crin – derived from the French word for horsehair, stiffening used to form hems usually found in millinery also known as horse hair braid.

D
Damask – a patterned woven fabric
Darts – a method of reducing fullness in a garment.
Double turned hem – a hem line that has been turned up twice
Duchesse Satin – a heavy weight satin with high sheen

E
Eyelets – small round holes used to lace up corset backed gowns, can be hand finished or created from metal.

F
Fish tail – a slim fitting gown that flares out from the knee.
Fitting – the method of adapting the garment to sit as desired to the body.
French Tack – a chain stitch by way of securing one or more pieces of fabric whilst retaining the movement.

G
Guipure – a very heavy weight lace

H
Habotai – a very light weight fabric used for scarves or linings.
Hanging loops – lengths of ribbon stitched into garments to allow them to be hung onto coat hangers.
Hems – the lower finishing of a garment.
Horse hair braid – see Crin.

I
Illusion neckline – fine mesh or tulle used to support 'floating detail over the shoulders, back or neck area
Interfacing – fabric usually with an adhesive backing used to stiffen collars, necklines etc.
Interlining – fabric used between the fashion fabric and lining to add stability.

J
Jacquard – a patterned woven fabric similar to Damask.

K

L
Lace – a mesh fabric that is characterised by cording or applique.
Lining – lightweight fabric used to finish a garment on the inside.

M
Mikado – polyester version of Zibeline – a heavily woven fabric with distinctive twill.
Modesty panel – a piece of fabric that preserves the modesty of the wearer either at the front or back of a neckline.

N
Net – a mesh fabric used extensively on bridal underskirts to produce fuller skirts.
Notch – a small snip in the fabric to mark fitting positions.

O

P
Pencil edging – an overlocked edge used to finish edges on hemlines and veils.
Petticoats – undergarments used to create fullness can be integral to the gown or worn separately. Fullness can be created either by a metal hoop or by tiered netting.
Piping – a method of finishing using bias cut fabric wrapped around a slender cord and stitched to necklines. Commonly used in soft furnishings.
Princess seams – vertical seams situated at the back and front of the garment either side of the centre front or centre back.

Q

R
Rat's tail – narrow satin cord used for fastening corsets.
Rolled hems – narrow double turned hems used extensively in bridal production.
Rouleau – a narrow tube of bias cut fabric, rouleaux plural referring to the loops made from this

S
Satin - luxurious fabric referring to the weave.
Side seams – seams of a garment situated at the side of the body.
Sink stitch – stitches sitting next to or sitting in a seam, also known as 'stitching in the ditch'.
Stay tape – slim pieces of fabric cut on the straight grain attached to seams where the bias may distort or stretch.

T
Tacking stitches – removable stitches temporarily holding the areas to be stitched – (Basting USA term).
Taffeta – a crisp fabric with a 'watermark' effect.
Tarlatan – loosely woven fabric used to interline garments
Train – the hem of a gown that falls behind the wearer and trails behind.
Tulle – lightweight netting used for wedding veils and skirts.

U
Understitching – stitching that holds facings in position.

V

W
Waist stay – elasticated or gross grain tape used to secure the bodice and prevent it from slipping below the waist area.

X

Y
Yolk – a piece of fabric that sits over the shoulders joining the back & front parts of a garment

Z
Zibeline – the silk version of Mikado fabric with distinctive twill weave.
Zipper – metal or plastic teeth methods of fastening garments

About the Author

S. L. Harbour first picked up a needle and thread aged just five, by the age of 14 she knew she wanted a career in sewing.

Following Art College and a Diploma in Fashion & Design she went on to spend over ten years employed in a couture bridal shop. Here she honed her dressmaking skills, working with brides on the shop floor, designing their perfect dress, pattern drafting and hand beading, lovingly stitching each gown.

In a career that spans over 25 years, Sarah has worked extensively with bridal shops supplying her valuable knowledge and skills to make each and every bride's day special with exquisitely fitted bridal gowns whether it be off the peg or a couture creation.

With bridal alterations becoming a coveted aspect of dressmaking, Sarah gives talks and mentors fellow dressmakers in the art of fitting and altering wedding dresses.

Bridal Alteration Techniques

Bridal Alteration Techniques is the book perhaps every dressmaker has been waiting for. The big sister to *'An Introduction to Bridal Alterations'* this book will delve deeper into the wonderful world of the bridal seamstress.

With over 25 years in the bridal industry both designing, making and altering bridal gowns S.L. Harbour brings a wealth of knowledge together in the only book of its kind from how to adjust laced edged hems to the much sought after skill of creating a corset back – a must for any dressmaker.

The book has full colour easy to follow instructions along with expert tips for working in the bridal industry. This invaluable book will enable the novice seamstress to move forward whilst offering the more experienced dressmaker another avenue from which to pursue a different and rewarding career.

Bridal Alteration Techniques by S.L. Harbour

ISBN: 978-1-9998840-0-0

Available exclusively through www.bridalalterationtechniques.co.uk

How to Open a Bridal Shop

Ever dreamed of opening your own bridal boutique?

Many start-up books will give blanket advice on retailing and owning your own business. There has never been anything specific to the bridal trade, this is because it is a very guarded industry and those who work in it wish to keep their secrets to themselves.

With over 250,000 weddings happening in the UK every year the market is huge but it is also highly competitive. Fashionista's who dream of opening their own wedding boutique will find the industry will close ranks and refuse to offer a helping hand to the novice.

No-one else will tell you the truth, the secrets or the little white lies of the Bridal Retail Business, but this book will be your Best Friend.

Within these pages you will discover;

~ How much Wedding Gowns really cost

~ Where you should buy your dresses from but more importantly where not to buy them from

~ Realistic start-up costs involved

~ Exclusivity

~ Staff training

~ Closing the sale

~ The Bridal Retail Calendar

And much, much more...

Available on Amazon Kindle

How to Open a Couture Bridal Shop – A Dressmaker's Guide

There comes a time in every dressmaker's life that the dream that one day they will make a bridal gown.

For some it is little more that day dream for others they may have been asked by a family member to create a loved one's dress. The very idea that a beautifully made bridal gown could be created by your very own hands, is this something that is obtainable? Is this something that could be turned into a business?

Yes it can be.

The bridal industry is changing; this time there is a new wave of bridal designers who can offer today's brides something new and something unique.

Bringing together a wealth of knowledge from working as a couture bridal seamstress and in retail S.L. Harbour talks you through the nitty gritty of owning a couture bridal shop.

The book includes essentials such as how to design a collection that works, the sizing element of couture bridal gowns, production deadlines and how to deal with them, pricing your work and the important factor of working with brides as they search for the dress of their dreams.

How to Open a Couture Bridal Shop – A Dressmaker's Guide Is a unique glimpse into the realms of couture bridal and a must for anyone considering opening their own bridal boutique.

Available on Amazon Kindle

How to Make a Bridal Bodice

This exciting new book comes complete with a couture bodice pattern and gives a step by step guide to creating both the manufactured and the couture bridal bodice.

Here S. L. Harbour shows how the same bodice can be created using two very different production methods.

With full colour images and detailed illustrations the book covers pattern lays, fabric choices, the use of boning and the all-important finishing techniques.

How to make a Bridal Bodice is an essential book for anyone wishing to expand their sewing skills and move on to producing their own couture bridal range.

Coming soon

Made in the USA
San Bernardino, CA
12 April 2019